PREP

PUSH

PIVOT

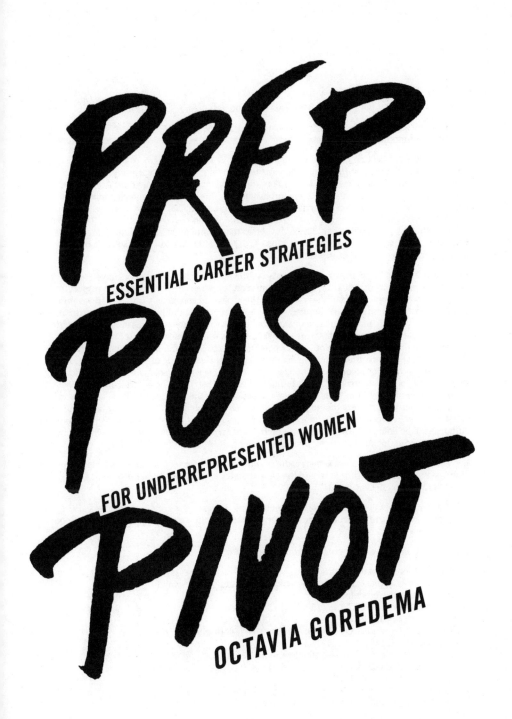

PREP
PUSH
PIVOT

ESSENTIAL CAREER STRATEGIES
FOR UNDERREPRESENTED WOMEN

OCTAVIA GOREDEMA

WILEY

Published by John Wiley & Sons, Inc., Hoboken, New Jersey.
Published simultaneously in Canada.

For general information on our other products and services or for technical support, please contact our Customer Care Department within the United States at (800) 762-2974, outside the United States at (317) 572-3993 or fax (317) 572-4002.

Wiley also publishes its books in a variety of electronic formats. Some content that appears in print may not be available in electronic formats. For more information about Wiley products, visit our website at www.wiley.com.

Library of Congress Cataloging-in-Publication Data:

Names: Goredema, Octavia, author.
Title: Prep, push, pivot : essential career strategies for underrepresented
    women / Octavia Goredema.
Description: Hoboken, NJ : Wiley, [2022] | Includes index.
Identifiers: LCCN 2021042426 (print) | LCCN 2021042427 (ebook) | ISBN
    9781119789079 (hardback) | ISBN 9781119789086 (adobe pdf) | ISBN
    9781119789093 (epub)
Subjects: LCSH: Minority women–Employment. | Vocational guidance.
Classification: LCC HD6057 .G67 2022 (print) | LCC HD6057 (ebook) | DDC
    331.4023–dc23/eng/20211012
LC record available at https://lccn.loc.gov/2021042426
LC ebook record available at https://lccn.loc.gov/2021042427

Cover design: Paul McCarthy

SKY10030307_120121

This book is dedicated to my daughters, Thalia and Marisa.

Contents

Introduction: My Commitment to Your Career

Women of color are the most underrepresented group in the corporate pipeline. We are hired at lower rates. We are promoted at lower rates. We are retained at lower rates. We are paid at lower rates.

Here's the irony. According to the United States Census Bureau, women of color are one of the fastest growing demographic groups in the United States. It has been projected that women of color will actually be the majority of all women here in the United States by 2060. But being a rapidly rising demographic isn't enough. We want opportunities. We want equal pay. We want promotions. We want to advance. What it takes to carve out a career is often debilitating and exhausting.

When the road is this long, and this steep, we need all the support we can get. You might be at the start of figuring out your career, or you might have a deep bench of experience coupled with a proven track record. At every stage, we need support. I wrote *Prep, Push, Pivot* to help you find that support and help you to reassess, determine, and pursue your goals as you build your career.

Every day, whether it's in group sessions with hundreds of employees or in a one-to-one coaching session, I help professionals figure out how to do their best work. I'm the founder of a career coaching company called Twenty Ten Agency. I became a career coach because I'm passionate about the things most people don't see: the mistakes, challenges, and experiences that come before success. I'm passionate about helping people reconnect with their potential. My work is centered on supporting people who want to advance but feel stuck.

Figuring out how to get unstuck is hard to do on your own, and not everyone has the opportunity to work directly with a coach. At Twenty Ten Agency, my team of coaches and I create career breakthroughs. Nothing makes me happier than hearing someone has finally achieved an important milestone. Our coaching is focused on understanding your values, getting real about obstacles, amplifying your potential, and reaching forward to pursue the next phase of your career.

I wrote this book because I want you to know your worth, use your voice, and identify the best ways to find and do your best work. Whether you're looking for a new job, dealing with losing one, pivoting into something new, or returning from a career break, *Prep, Push, Pivot* delivers strategies to help you advance. This book is divided into three sections:

Part I is focused on preparation. These first three chapters of *Prep* lay the foundation for knowing your worth, cementing your career values, bouncing back if you lose a job, and securing the salary you deserve when you land a new one.

Part II is centered on pushing forward. Over the course of three chapters, *Push* helps you position yourself for a promotion, navigate a career break, and figure out how to align your career goals if you're also a caregiver.

Part III guides you through pivotal professional milestones. These final three chapters, *Pivot*, address how to plan for a career change, discuss how to pay it forward, and provide an array of resources to help you achieve your next big milestone.

Some of the stories shared in this book are based on composite accounts of women who faced specific circumstances during their careers. Coaching conversations are strictly confidential, so the stories I share have been created with fictious details. But the perspectives and experiences shared in these stories derive from the opportunities, concerns, challenges, and accomplishments of women I've encountered who are striving to push forward.

You'll also find Q&A sections within the book, sharing the frequent questions I've addressed during numerous coaching sessions and workshops. If you'd like to dig deeper, head to octaviagoredema.com where you will find a collection of *Prep, Push, Pivot* resources to help you accelerate.

Knowing how to navigate your career at pivotal moments can be scary, lonely, and hard. The stakes are usually high, and we're often left to figure things out on our own. I wrote this book because I have one mission—to propel you forward. *Prep, Push, Pivot* is designed to help you achieve your goals at every stage of your career

Know your worth. Land your next opportunity. Pay it forward. Never settle.

Let's get started.

PREP
PUSH
PIVOT

PART I
PREP

CHAPTER 1

Know Your Worth

Building your career is the most valuable, and the most personal, investment you'll ever make.

Navigating your career as a woman of color in the workplace, however, continues to be an uphill struggle. We are the fastest growing demographic group in the United States,[1] but we are the most underrepresented group in the corporate pipeline. As a career coach, I have one mission—to help you move forward.

Knowing your worth underpins everything. Your worth will be tested by the systemic inequities that women of color face every single day.

I know how important it is to cement your career values because it took me a long time to figure this out for myself. I started my career just over two decades ago. Landing my first job after graduating from my university started a rollercoaster that has included being promoted, leading teams, international relocations, taking a career break, returning to work as a parent, and making a career pivot.

It took me a long time to realize my career values were the foundation for everything. Countless times, I found myself in roles or situations that did not support my values. Despite this, I endeavored to do my best work, and yet even when I delivered results it just didn't feel right. In the past, the only time I considered my worth was when I was asked to prepare for a performance review. Even then, it was a struggle to self-assess my skills, and I calculated my worth through my employer's lens versus my own. Over the course of my career, I've created and pursued professional goals, but there were also hard times when I felt lost and uncertain of what I should be aiming for. By discounting what mattered most, I was working hard, but without a true purpose.

So, what exactly is your worth? For many of us, it's how much we earn, but in truth your worth runs way deeper than that. It's about understanding what enables you to do your best work, defining your nonnegotiables for your career, and embracing your unlocked potential.

As a first step, I'd like you to cement your career values, as this provides the foundation for the professional goals you will pursue.

Cement Your Career Values

Your career values are your guiding light, in good times and tough times. They underpin everything. Jobs will come and go, bosses and coworkers will come and go, but your values remain—and they are unique to you.

Remember, you have choices, and when it comes to your career you decide what matters most. I recommend documenting your career values using the following question prompts and reviewing and refining your responses several times a year. This makes your values a priority.

Your career values encompass the following core principles:

■ Your achievements
■ Your purpose
■ Your inspiration
■ Your style of work
■ Your mission
■ Your reputation

Career values provide the foundation for you to create goals that align with your purpose and principles. In chapter 9, you will find a worksheet you can use to save your responses to the following questions:

1. What matters most to you personally when it comes to your career?
2. What's on your must-have list when it comes to the work you do next?
3. What makes you feel excited and inspired about your work?
4. What motivates you to do your best work?
5. What are you naturally good at?
6. What would you love to do more of at work?
7. What energizes and excites you?
8. What type of environments do you want to work in?
9. What's your preferred work schedule?
10. Is there anything that's nonnegotiable for you at work?
11. What are the greatest accomplishments of your career?
12. What is it about the accomplishments that make them special for you?
13. What do you want your career to feel like?
14. What do you want to be known for?
15. How do you measure success?

When you start to think about your career values, your responses to the questions may require deeper and longer reflection, and your responses may change or evolve over time. There are no right or wrong answers and it's not a test. Your responses are for you to define. This is a space for you to consider what matters most in your career so that you can build a platform for goal setting and actions that will get you closer to where you want to be.

Get Your Goals Ready

Most people are asked about their goals roughly once a year when the performance review cycle rolls around. Somewhere in the self-assessment form you're asked to complete for your supervisor there will be a question along the lines of "What do you want to accomplish in the next year?" or "What do you want to be doing five years from now?"

Some of us may be tempted to answer, "I want to be working somewhere else" or "I want to have your job and your salary." Most of us panic a little about the question and try to figure out an acceptable and appropriate answer. Whether it's a performance review that's looming or your own personal thought process, considering our future can be scary because we just don't know. Being asked about goals can feel like the worst kind of test.

- "Can I be honest?"
- "Am I thinking too small?"
- "Is my goal too big and unachievable?"
- "I straight up don't know what I'm aiming for."

These are legitimate thoughts when someone asks you about your career goals. Goals are powerful, complex, and captivating things. They can be exhilarating and terrifying, all rolled into one.

So, what happens if you're confused about possible career goals? Or maybe you know what you want, but you don't know how to get there.

How to Set Goals

After you've documented and reviewed your career values, it's the perfect time to align your goals. If you're not sure where to start, pick a goal that really excites you, or could be a stepping-stone to something that really excites you.

Some of your goals might be big, some might be smaller, but there are no rights or wrongs when it comes to what you decide on. It just needs to feel right. The only thing I ask is to push yourself out of your comfort zone. That can be hard at first, and it may take a few attempts. I shared a set of goals with one of my mentors once and his immediate response was, "That sounds great, Octavia, but I'd like you to dream bigger." That one statement alone was transformative to me. So, I added another layer to my goals that were bigger than I'd ever contemplated. He was right. After all, if you'd told me I'd start my career in one country and build it in another, I'd never have believed it.

Here are some questions to help you get started:

1. Based on your career values, what do you want to experience in the next chapter of your career?
2. Where do you feel stuck?
3. What do you want to set in motion?
4. What skills do you want to develop?
5. What's a next step that's just out of reach?
6. What's a next step that would feel like a giant leap?

How to Stay on Track

When you've chosen a goal to pursue, start to outline the next steps you need to take to make this goal happen. Often, professionals I work with assign a deadline to a goal, for example:

"I want to secure a new role by the end of the calendar year."

As a coach, I think it's fantastic that you have a time line in mind for what you want. However, I always recommend focusing on the time frames to the actions you will take to pursue your goal. For example, the steps you need to take to do that might include updating your résumé, talking to your network about opportunities, and of course, spending time looking at job postings. Assigning time frames for key tasks, or including the frequency for key tasks, is what will propel you forward.

Including when you will do the tasks creates an action plan, which could look like this:

- "Create an updated version of my résumé by the end of the month."
- "Set aside time twice a week to reach out to people in my network to ask for advice about my search."
- "Allocate Sunday afternoons as uninterrupted time to review job postings and prepare applications."

I believe the best way to stay on track with your goals is to focus entirely on the actions you need to take. We can't control the outcome of our actions, but we can control what we do. By scheduling time for the actions required, and doing them, you may land that new job before the end of the calendar year, or after the end of the calendar year, but you will be moving forward constantly.

Sometimes our goal seems so far removed from our current reality that we don't know where to start. When that happens, it's not uncommon to feel deflated or even downsize our visions to something more achievable. This why breaking the big, scary goal into smaller pieces and scheduling the steps is so crucial. Setting your intentions to pursue the goal is the secret to success. Goals will only become accomplishments if you act. The best way to do that is to just start. Don't worry about what comes next; just take it one step at a time.

Create a strategy to hold yourself accountable, especially during the tough times. Maybe you choose to tag team with a friend, where you each share a goal you're working on and give each other encouragement along the way. Perhaps you journal about your process. Maybe you work with a career coach. Or perhaps you schedule time on your calendar to act and plan your next steps. Do whatever works for you.

When you've decided on and scheduled your next steps, you should plan how you'll celebrate each step. Yes, I advocate celebrating every step, not just reaching the end of the goal. It could be something small, like reserving time to do something you love or something bigger, like treating yourself to a special purchase. You get to decide. This will reinforce that you're making a continuous investment in your professional development and signifies that every step matters.

Here are some questions to help you stay on track with your goal:

1. How important is this goal to you?
2. What ideas do you have about next steps?
3. How could you break the next steps down into smaller pieces?
4. What's the next action you should take?
5. Who can you ask for help with this?
6. How will I celebrate the completion of each step?
7. What will you commit to doing next?

As a final step, use your career values and goals to create your own road map. This is something you can revisit every quarter and adjust and update as you need to. In chapter 9 you will find a blank Career Road Map worksheet for you to use.

Your Career Road Map should include:

- Your career values
- Milestone moments so far
- Short-term goals
- Longer-term goals
- Ideas for how to progress
- Ideas for how you will celebrate

Career Road Map

Use your career values and goals to create your own road map.

MY CAREER VALUES

Do work that channels my creativity.

Collaborate on exciting projects with talented professionals.

Become respected in my industry for my skills.

MILESTONE MOMENTS

Landing my first promotion.

Seeing my first campaign launch and gain traction.

SHORT-TERM GOALS	LONGER-TERM GOALS
Gather assets from previous campaigns and update my digital portfolio.	Complete my certification.

HOW TO PROGRESS	HOW TO CELEBRATE
Dedicate one day a month to professional development. Find a mentor.	Invest in new equipment.

Figure 1.1

Channel all your energy into taking those steps toward the career you're building. One step at a time. Focus on what you can control: your own actions.

Decide that if there are obstacles standing in your way and impeding your goals, you will do everything in your power to push them out of the way. Commit to asking, more than once, for what you want. If that doesn't work, commit to finding an opportunity that meets your needs.

Aggregating Your Accomplishments

My coaching clients already know that this topic is something I constantly talk about. Aggregating your accomplishments is everything when it comes to knowing your worth. If you're not sure what I'm referring to, then it's likely you have some work to do, but I promise it will be worth it.

Basically, it's easy to forget our accomplishments. Even if we don't intend to. We do stuff, we get busy, we do more stuff, we pause for a minute when something major happens, and then we move on to the next thing. That's life, I get it, but I want you to stop. Yes, stop right now and answer this question:

> *What are the 12 most important things that you achieved in the last year?*
>
> If you already have a list, congratulations! My next question for you is, how often do you update it and how often do you review it?
>
> If you aren't in the habit of tracking your accomplishments regularly, I'd like you to adopt a new habit, starting today. I'm serious about this, because I believe documenting your accomplishments is the single most important thing anyone can do for their career. So, with that in mind, do whatever it takes: start

a document on your desktop, create a list on your phone, start journaling, build a brag book. Call it whatever you want and do whatever you need to do to remind yourself that you know your stuff.

When something great happens—big or small—write it down in a dedicated space that is just for your accomplishments. That way, it's easy to revisit when you need to. At the end of each week, look at it. At the end of each month, reflect on everything and pick the number one win that stands out. If you do that every month, you'll have a least 12 amazing things to reflect on one year from now.

Dealing with Career Envy

We've all been there. You happen to catch a notification on LinkedIn from a former colleague who's suddenly scored an unbelievable promotion, or an incredible new role, and your heart starts to sink. In an age of constant social media updates, it can feel like others are accelerating way faster than you are. Career envy happens to the best of us, even when we're happy for the people with good news to share.

If you find yourself starting to compare and question your progress, it's time to switch gears and embrace your achievements and goals without the filter of anyone else to cloud your view. If that feels uncomfortable, perhaps because you can't shake the perception that someone else is moving ahead faster, remember this one fact. Even if you both started at the exact same point with the exact same skills, your journeys will not be the same, and that's OK.

Despite knowing the person whose career you're coveting, you may not know everything about their back story, or the reality of their career journey. The accomplishments that look fabulous and exhilarating from the outside can be stressful and unfulfilling on the inside. All we know is how our own career path feels, and that's where we need to focus attention. Instead of comparing yourself to others, focus on what you're building toward. Use the achievements of others as fuel to motivate you positively; if they can do cool things, you can and will too.

Working Through Challenges

Watching women of color successfully climb the corporate ladder is always inspiring because there are so few of us that make it. As a result, this type of ascent often makes headlines. Each time someone defies convention to make it to the corner office, the boardroom, the Senate, or wherever they've set their intent, we collectively cheer and applaud from the sidelines. But as we celebrate, I often reflect on what we don't know, or may not see. We don't know the struggle that preceded the achievement, or how it feels to be the first, only, or one of just a few, after a ceiling has been broken. Who picks up the pieces?

A few years ago, I heard US Vice President Kamala Harris say this, and her words stuck with me for the longest time:

> *"When we talk about breaking barriers, some would suggest that you're just on this side of the barrier and then you turn out on this side of the barrier. No, it's breaking barriers. And when you break things, it hurts."*[2]

As women of color navigating the workplace, we see and feel barriers to advancing that are largely invisible to white professionals. Breaking barriers is painful. Then, if we persist and push through, it can be equally painful on the other side. How your career looks on the outside isn't anything like how it feels.

My work is centered on helping others overcome challenges in the workplace. No one is immune from facing challenges at work; even professionals who are perceived as highfliers will have periods where they struggle. If you're facing a hard time, you're not alone, and you will come through it.

During my career there were periods of time when I was the only Black woman in a meeting, the only Black woman on my team, and the only Black woman in the building. When you're the only, the first, or one of very few, there's an inherent pressure to be perfect, because you represent your race and gender, not just your job title. And on top of that, it often feels like there's no protection.

The Devastating Effects of Discrimination

Despite decades of anti-discrimination laws, being a woman of color in the workplace exerts a largely unseen emotional tax on your performance, well-being, and ability to thrive. A recent study by Catalyst, a nonprofit that advocates for accelerating and advancing women into leadership, found that 68 percent of people of color are on guard to protect against bias and unfair treatment within their work teams.[3] Most of us know we don't need a survey to tell us what we have already experienced. Studies repeatedly show that invisibility and exclusion—often described as the feeling of not being heard or recognized in group settings—is a widespread problem for women of color.[4]

While many of us have become accustomed to the perils of unconscious bias, lack of support, and performative allyship, dealing with insensitive language, microaggressions, harassment, and discrimination is one of the most devastating experiences for anyone to navigate in their place of work.

Knowing your worth, even in the face of the steepest of challenges, is paramount. At the federal level, laws protect employees from unfair treatment because of their race, sex, religion, national origin, age, and disability status. These categories also cover discrimination based on color, gender identity, pregnancy, and sexual orientation. In addition, many states provide more expansive discrimination protections. For example, in 2019 California became the first state in the United States to ban employers and school officials from discriminating against people based on their natural hair.[5] Governor Gavin Newsom signed the Crown Act into law, making it illegal to enforce dress codes or grooming policies against hairstyles such as afros, braids, twists, and locs.

If you are being harassed or discriminated against, document the experiences detailing the date, time, and location the incident took place, what was said or took place, and if there were witnesses. Talk to an employment lawyer who can provide advice, and explain your options based on your experience. This may include reporting the issue to your employer, filing a complaint with the US Equal Employment Opportunity Commission, or filing a lawsuit.

Microaggressions are defined as everyday slights, indignities, put-downs, and insults that members of marginalized groups experience in their day-to-day interactions.[6] If you've been on the receiving end of one, or heard one, you know it. It's toxic, it's disrespectful, and it's wrong. Examples of microaggressions can include:

- An assumption of lesser employment status
- Being mistaken for someone else of the same racial background
- Being ignored
- Questions about background, such as being asked, "Where are you from?"
- Discriminatory comments disguised as compliments
- Using racially insensitive language
- Touching of hair

Microaggressions have an impact on your self-esteem, job satisfaction, mental health, and physical health, so it's critical for you to decide where to draw the line, however hard that may be. Kevin Nadal, professor of psychology at John Jay College, developed a tool kit called the *Guide to Responding to Microaggressions*.[7] It lists five questions to ask yourself when weighing the consequences of responding to a microaggression:

1. If I respond, could my physical safety be in danger?
2. If I respond, will the person become defensive and will this lead to an argument?
3. If I respond, how will this affect my relationship with this person?
4. If I don't respond, will I regret not saying something?
5. If I don't respond, does that convey that I accept the behavior or statement?

Dealing with discrimination, harassment, or microaggressions in the workplace is deeply distressing; don't go it alone. Lean on friends, family, and mental health resources and specialists as and when needed. We did not create these workplace land mines and we cannot solve them alone. It's hard to change anyone's behavior if they don't want to change. It's not possible to single-handedly change your workplace culture. But you can control your responses and actions and safeguard your mental health.

Bad Bosses and Coworkers

A few years ago, while leading a career advancement workshop, I said, "Raise your hand if you've encountered a bad boss." I quickly realized I should have said, "Raise your hand if you've never had a bad boss." It seems that bad bosses, sadly, are everywhere. I'm not quite sure how this happens, but when it does, it's jarring. If you're dealing with a faltering relationship with your supervisor, it's tough. When trust breaks down, it's damaging on both sides. Broken trust causes stress, and it can affect your productivity, performance, and morale, which in turn will likely make the relationship even worse.

If you don't know what to do, there's one thing I want you to remember. Don't let a bad manager derail your ambition, career values, or goals. Maintaining perspective is crucial, but not always easy if your emotions are running high. Take a step back and assess whether the poor dynamic and behavior reflect your corporate culture *or* can be sourced directly to the individual. Understanding the bigger picture and the underlying causes will help guide how best to approach and respond to the situation.

Your boss may or may not be aware of the negative impact their approach has on others. However, when your work is affected by the behavior of someone more senior than you, it's crucial to protect and nurture what matters most: your professional development. If your personalities clash, the emphasis is on you, as a direct report, to adapt to your boss's preferred style. Observe how your supervisor works and consider how you may be able to adapt in response. This may not be easy, but it's a good place to start.

However, if the situation is truly toxic, trust your gut. If the relationship feels beyond repair, trust the feeling, and know when enough is enough. Toxicity will rapidly erode your well-being, and if it gets to that point, it's time to prioritize your needs and find an opportunity that allows you to thrive.

Dealing with bad coworkers can be just as tricky. The ripples created from just one challenging coworker can affect not just you, but an entire team. It can feel like a lose-lose situation. If you try to ignore them, the behavior could just keep going; if you address it, it could cause conflict with no guarantee of a resolution.

The first thing to do is set boundaries and do whatever you can to prevent your coworker from consuming your energy. To help maintain boundaries, and your sanity, talk to someone you trust. That person can help you brainstorm strategies for dealing with your bad coworker based on your goals and needs. As and when it happens, document the bad behavior so that you have a list of evidence just in case things escalate. If your coworker's behavior is impinging on more than one person, you and your colleagues should consider collectively talking to a manager.

If the coworker is someone who reports to you, it's important to capture each instance in writing as it happens for your own records, including the date and time. You will need to provide evidence of the poor performance, actions, or bad habits as you work to resolve the issue with your employee. Your company's policies and procedures, and counsel from HR, will provide the guidance you need if the poor performance continues.

Schedule time to talk to your direct report in private and listen intently. You need to be transparent about how their behavior has a negative impact on performance. Give constructive feedback with specific examples, but remember, the discussion needs to be a two-way street. This is your opportunity to learn what may be causing the problem. Listen carefully to what the person you manage has to say. There may be legitimate issues, such as unintentionally unclear direction from you, pressing personal problems, bureaucratic constraints, or lack of sufficient training that's causing the situation. To move forward, set clear expectations and put a plan in writing to resolve the issue. Offer support along the way, monitor how things are going, and follow up to review progress together.

Coworkers and bosses will change over time and you'll rarely have complete control of team dynamics. Your career and how you choose to work, however, should consistently remain your top priority. Choose to stay on track with your goals. If you're struggling to make it work, take time to figure out the best way to move forward, either in this role or in a new one.

Overcoming Imposter Syndrome

No one feels confident constantly. Whether you're the intern, the CEO, or somewhere in between, your confidence can sometimes take a hit when you need it the most. Work is called work for a reason. It's hard. It's tough if you feel others are advancing while you're wracked with self-doubt.

If you're suffering from a crisis of career confidence, identifying approaches to reframe your thought patterns will go a long way. If you find yourself undermining your experience, questioning your accomplishments, or feeling uncomfortable with recognition, you may be experiencing imposter syndrome. The term was coined by psychologists Dr. Suzanne Imes and Dr. Pauline Rose Clance in the 1970s. Imes and Clance identified a phenomenon occurring among high achievers who are unable to internalize and accept their success. Those affected often attribute their accomplishments to luck rather than to ability and fear that others will eventually unmask them as a fraud.[8]

Imposter syndrome is prevalent, and almost everyone experiences it at some point. Being aware of this doesn't necessarily make the feelings go away. My advice as a coach, and as someone who also deals with imposter syndrome on a regular basis, is to acknowledge the feeling but do your best not to let it hold you back. Don't let doubt control your actions. Talk it out with someone you trust. Release the pressure valve and alleviate the pursuit of perfection. This doesn't mean you should stop striving to do your best. Instead, you need to focus your mind on setting yourself up for success. A great way to kick-start this is to remember what you do well and what you've achieved in the past. When you're feeling low, it can be easy to forget all the great things you've done in the past.

Recognize and fully embrace your expertise and your accomplishments over the course of your career so far. We need to do this whether we're feeling inadequate or riding high. Your feelings about work can and will fluctuate, but your accomplishments are concrete. Don't forget them. Negative thoughts can snowball if you're feeling down, so if you feel your confidence is plummeting take time out and remind yourself of what you're great at and where you've been successful in the past.

Coping with Burnout

Even if you haven't put a label on it, chances are you will experience burnout more than once in your career. How it manifests—and how it feels—can affect each of us in different ways. Warning signs can include an increasingly negative attitude or apathy toward your work, constant exhaustion, anxiety, insomnia, and feelings of ineffectiveness.

Asking for help and admitting you're struggling can seem scary, but don't be afraid to do it. If you don't take steps to take care of your health and well-being, your ability to deliver great work will fly out of the window. Take a break and talk to someone you trust. Recognizing and sharing how you're feeling is a vital first step. Work with your supervisor to get on your priorities. If you've been working around the clock, revise your schedule and give yourself time to adapt to a different way of working.

Ensuring you're getting enough sleep will pay dividends, as it's the gateway to increased productivity, happiness, and smarter decision making. Slow down and make space for things that make you feel good during your workday. Reconfiguring old habits takes time, but stick with it. When you start to feel better, don't revert to old habits; make sure you're putting your well-being front and center, as well as your deadlines.

When I was growing up, my mother told me that I'd have to work twice as hard as everyone else to get ahead. I listened to her advice, and where possible, I tried my hardest to follow it. However, after several years I started to realize working hard and waiting for your boss to notice isn't enough. That will only get you so far. And working twice as hard over the course of a career just isn't healthy, or sustainable. It's important to recognize when enough is enough. Your health and well-being should be your top priority.

Knowing your worth, even when it's not reflected at you, is pivotal. Understand that it's okay to fail or make mistakes, even when you feel you don't have space to do so, and that this is part of building a career. You will stumble. You will mess something up. You will hear "no," or deal with not being noticed at all. But keep going regardless.

Align your actions with your ambition. Make sure whatever you're doing at work is getting you closer to where you want to be. If you know you can do better, commit to aiming higher. When dealing with challenges in the workplace, lean hard on a support system—this may include friends, people you trust in your network, a mentor, or a coach. Don't go it alone.

But remember, no one else will be truly invested in your career from start to finish, which is why you must continually invest in yours. The following chapters will guide you on how to do just that.

Q&A

Here are some questions I've been asked about career values, goals, and challenges at work.

I have a goal, but I'm struggling to make progress; what do I do?

If your heart is still set on achieving your goal, breaking it down into smaller pieces is the best place to start. It feels too immense, you'll start to panic.

If you're like me, there are times when there's an important task you know you must do, but you'll find almost anything else to do instead. Remind yourself why the task is important, use visual cues if you can that cement in your mind why you're doing this in the first place. Then, the most effective and efficient thing to do is to develop a "procrastination antidote" that gets you on track.

Your system could be sharing your progress with a friend, or keeping a calendar on your wall, or tracking next steps in an app. Try whatever it takes. For me personally, removing any distractions so I can focus on what I need to do works every time. This involves ignoring e-mail, turning off my phone, and just diving in. If it helps, create a personal incentive as a reward for finally getting the task done and off your to-do-list.

After you rip off the bandage and just start, you'll usually find your task wasn't as scary as you feared it would be. Often our minds inflate the task to be bigger, scarier, or more laborious than it really is. So, find the antidote that will get you started, because the sooner you start, the sooner you'll be on your way.

I like my job, but my boss is a micromanager, and I'm worried he's holding me back. What should I do?

The fact you're enjoying your role and want to advance is fantastic. With that foundation in place, you can still progress, even with a micromanager as a boss. The first thing you need to determine is how your boss feels about your performance. Have you had a performance review? What was the feedback? If your boss is happy with your work, his tendency to micromanage may be a character trait versus a reflection on you.

Micromanagers have specific characteristics, and it's likely you're one of many people who are affected by their challenging work style. Try not to let it get you down. Instead, focus on the positive elements of your job that you find rewarding, skills you are learning, or the networks and experience you are building.

While it's painful to endure, remember you won't be stuck with your micromanaging boss forever. Anticipate your boss's needs but continue to do your best work and maintain a positive attitude. If there's something specific you need to support your professional development, talk to your boss about it and listen carefully to the response. Creating a dialogue about your future goals, and how you can do your best work, is a positive thing to do.

I hate my job, but I'm afraid if I start a new job, it will be just as bad. What do I do?

If you don't like something at work, you have options. No one should stay in a situation that's not working for them. The important thing is to be clear on what you do want. Spend time reviewing your responses to the Career Values questions. They will help you identify if there are ways you could make some positive changes in your current role. If that's not possible, your career values are like a compass: they'll show the direction you need to move toward.

Deciding is liberating. When you know what you need in the next phase of your career, plan with intent and start thinking about who can help you figure out the steps you're unsure of. Between friends, their friends, the Internet, books, podcasts, and social media, there's a deep bench of people, tools, and resources you can leverage to help you prepare for your next opportunity.

Your career values will also help you as you work through the interview process during your job search. You will have already decided what you want, and what your nonnegotiables are. That insight, coupled with your experiences in your current role, means you're unlikely to end up in an identical situation to the one you're in now. Things can—and will—get better.

How to Bounce Back When You Lose Your Job

Losing your job is traumatic. Even if you saw it coming. If you didn't see it coming, well, that's a whole other experience. Losing a job happens to so many of us, but when it happens to you it really, really hurts. Dealing with the impact on your finances, self-esteem, and relationships can feel like an avalanche of angst. And that's before you embark on what's needed to find the next role.

You are not your job. But how we earn our money matters, and our work is a crucial part of our identity. Although it's hard to have perspective in the moment, I know through my work as a career coach that losing your job can be a launching pad to so much more. Your period of unemployment won't last forever, but not knowing how long it will take to land your next position can be truly terrifying.

On top of this, other out-of-your-control factors can come into play. The state of the economy dictates the supply and demand for roles in your chosen field; hence, you will may face increased competition for fewer and fewer opportunities during a downturn. In addition, studies have shown time and again that minority populations are hit the hardest by unemployment levels during recessions.

If a sudden loss of income triggers an immediate threat to your survival, the combination of unemployment and the systemic challenges of being a woman of color can make a horrible situation feel perilous. Your stress levels hit a peak, which in turn has the potential to upend your mental and physical well-being. Most of the time our bodies know how to deal with stress in small doses, but chronic stress over a prolonged period can contribute to long-term health problems.

Bouncing back may not happen overnight, but that doesn't mean it isn't going to happen at all. You will come through it. When you feel like everything is spinning out of control, the one thing you can hold on to is this: You ultimately have total control of your next steps, and as you pursue those, a good attitude and concerted effort will be invaluable. It will be hard, but regardless of your level of experience or the size and depth of your network, the most important person in all this is you. And you will have to push yourself because no one else is going to do it for you.

Through my work as a career coach, I've witnessed scores of people at various stages of their careers bounce back from losing a job. I've taken what worked for them to create a set of recommendations and approaches to help you.

This chapter will help you navigate the next steps for finding your next role after suddenly losing your job.

Jennifer's Story ————————————

Jennifer didn't see it coming. She was seven weeks into her new job and finally starting to get a handle on how things worked. It hadn't been easy, but Jennifer's friends kept reminding her that the first few weeks anywhere would be sticky and in a little while she would be settled in.

When she logged in for her weekly one-to-one with her manager, Jennifer was stunned to see he wasn't alone. The HR manager, who had sent her offer letter, was also in the video conference. Jennifer was let go for not meeting the requirements of her role. Ten minutes later, she found herself aimlessly staring at a blank screen, not knowing what to think or what to do next.

For a week, Jennifer didn't tell a soul. She lived alone, so it was an easy secret to keep. Then, her mom called and happened to ask how her job was going. Jennifer didn't want to lie, and her mom's response was exactly what she'd anticipated. Disappointment. Jennifer hated the idea of anyone knowing she'd been fired. She was so excited when she had landed her new job that she'd told everyone. Not only was she in a more senior role, but Jennifer had also joined a company she'd admired for a long time. At the end of the first week, she had proudly announced her new role across all her social media accounts and her phone hadn't stopped buzzing for the rest of that night.

Now, two months later, Jennifer just wanted to hide. She didn't know how to explain to the people in her network that she'd been fired. She felt like a failure.

"You're Fired." ————————————

No one wants to hear those words, even if you secretly want out from your job. Let's be frank, getting fired is humiliating because it happens when your position is terminated with cause.

From an employment law perspective, employers rarely go into the detail on the reasons for a termination, for liability or risk management reasons.

If you were fired due to a performance issue, or because you did something that was grounds for dismissal, commit to your professional development and turn your mistakes into a growth opportunity. Get real about your strengths and your weaknesses. Identify where you need to do work when it comes to performance issues or traits that have derailed you. Invest in your professional development with books, podcasts, workshops, courses, or coaching.

If you were not the right fit for the organization, reflect on what you've learned from the experience so that you'll be able to apply those insights as you plan your next steps. In the moment though, I know it can be devastating. If you find yourself in this situation, I want you to remember this: your life is not over. Decide what you will do differently moving forward and commit to it. Getting fired is an opportunity to hit the reset button. Good things happen after a reset if you learn from the experience. It won't define you forever.

"This Just Didn't Work Out."

Being terminated can be devastating as it can happen without warning. If you're an at-will employee, your employer can terminate your role at any time for any reason, or for no reason, without incurring legal liability. Likewise, an at-will employee is free to leave a job at any time for any or no reason with no adverse legal consequences.[1]

It is important, however, to flag that federal and state governments have laws protecting at-will employees from wrongful termination. These laws protect employees and job applicants against discrimination, harassment, and unfair treatment in the workplace because of race, religion, gender, pregnancy, age, disability, sexual orientation, marital status, and other protected factors.[2]

If you have been terminated, you should agree on your departure language with your employer. Ask how they plan to announce your departure internally and externally. Where possible, work together on mutually agreeable language that you will both use as needed. Remember, most employers don't provide the reason for an employee's departure; if asked by a prospective employer, it's common practice to provide just the date of hire, departure, and confirmation of job.

"You're Being Furloughed."

A furlough is a mandatory, temporary unpaid leave of absence. Furloughs can happen due to lack of work or your employer's financial constraints. If you find out you're being furloughed, you will have to stop working, or reduce your hours, and wait to hear what happens next. This can feel excruciating because the outcome is out of your hands.

Furloughs can take different forms and they are used by companies in the face of challenging circumstances. When the situation improves, companies can then bring their employees back. Sometimes, however, furloughs can become layoffs.

Furloughs are meant to be short-term arrangements, but the duration can vary. If you're being furloughed, you may be required to take a certain number of unpaid hours over a set time, take a specified number of unpaid days or hours throughout the year, or take a single block of unpaid time.[3]

When you're furloughed, you cannot perform any tasks related to your role and you don't get paid. Workers are not allowed to work for their employer during the furlough period. It's a tough and uncertain time. Not only is your paycheck immediately affected, but you're in limbo while you wait with fingers crossed for a more hopeful outcome.

Some companies maintain health care benefits during the furlough period; however, some may not. Some states allow furloughed employees to collect unemployment benefits; some don't. During the COVID-19 pandemic, however, the government enhanced eligibility for unemployment benefits at a federal level. If you're uncertain of your benefit options, talk to your HR team and check out your state's unemployment benefits website, which has helpful and up-to-date information regarding unemployment benefits.

"You're Being Laid Off."

If you're laid off, it's a result of your company's performance as opposed to your own. According to the Society for Human Resource Management, the term "layoff" is mostly used to describe a type of termination where the employee holds no blame.[4] It can be completely devastating to lose an opportunity due to circumstances beyond your control. Your security has been stripped away and you're suddenly faced with finding a new job.

Sometimes layoffs are temporary. An employer may have reason to believe or hope it will be able to recall workers back to work from a layoff, although it may end up being a permanent situation. (In contrast to layoffs, a reduction in force occurs when a position is eliminated with no intention of replacing it and results in a permanent cut in headcount.[5])

Companies may offer severance packages in connection with layoffs or reductions in force, but they are not required to. If you are offered a severance package, take your time to review the terms on which the severance is being offered to you before you sign any paperwork.

"Am I Dealing with a Wrongful Termination?"

To be wrongfully terminated means you have been fired for an illegal reason. This may involve the violation of federal, state, or local anti-discrimination laws, or whistleblower or anti-retaliation laws. For example, as an employee you cannot be fired because of your race, gender, ethnic background, religion, or disability. It's also illegal for someone to be fired if they lodged a legal complaint against their employer, participated in an investigation into illegal conduct, or brought the employer's wrongdoing to light as a whistleblower. This is considered retaliation and would put your employer in breach of the law.[6]

In addition, if you have a written employment contract, you should review if your termination violates the terms of that contract. If that is the case, it would entitle you to damages for breach of contract. If you think you may have a legal claim against your employer, you should speak to an attorney as soon as possible. In chapter 1 I discuss the devastating effects of discrimination. If you are dealing with unlawful workplace behavior it's vital to seek the support you need, both legally and personally. Wrongful termination may be covered by federal, state, or local laws that prohibit employment discrimination, and by contract law if your employer breached an employment agreement or the company violated its own policy by terminating your employment.

An attorney will help you determine what remedies are available and what recourse you may have. Many lawyers offer free consultations and will be able to tell you whether you have a case. Legal counsel is crucial to help determine the best course of action based on your specific circumstances.

Understanding the Terms of Your Departure

If you're being let go, your employer will provide you with the terms of your departure. Common agreements can include:

- Severance pay terms
- Vacation payout terms
- Benefits information
- Return of property requirements
- Non-compete or non-solicit requirements
- Confidentiality and non-disclosure agreements
- Unemployment information
- Career transition services
- A general release of claims and covenant not to sue

Your employer will provide you with a list of any benefits you're entitled to and guidance on how to access them. They will also specify the return of any company property, and you are likely to be asked to sign legal documents. Remember, you are not obligated to sign anything immediately. Take time to review everything carefully. It's important that you understand the terms and clarify any questions. If you are offered a severance package, it usually requires you to relinquish certain rights, whether those rights are known to you or not. The decision is ultimately yours. You may choose to accept and sign or to decline.

Companies will often offer severance packages to laid-off employees; however, this not guaranteed. Most employees are not automatically entitled to severance. Employers usually offer it in exchange for the terminated employee signing an agreement that waives any rights or grounds for a lawsuit against the employer.

Speak up if you're unclear about anything related to your departure terms. There's a lot to take in, and it's important to ask if there's anything you're unsure of. Some components of a severance package may be up for negotiation. There's no guarantee, but it can't hurt to ask.

If you've been fired, it's unlikely you will be offered a severance package and, in addition, you may not be entitled to unemployment benefits. The laws on this vary from state to state. The US Department of Labor's unemployment insurance programs provide unemployment benefits to eligible workers who become unemployed through no fault of their own and meet certain other eligibility requirements. In most states, this means you need to have separated from your last job due to a lack of available work.[7]

If your employer offers career transition services as part of a departure agreement, my advice is to use whatever you can access. The services are often offered with a specific time frame. Career transition assistance from employers can sometimes include one-to-one coaching, workshops, learning resources, and job search strategy training.

If you need clarity on the provisions of your departure agreement, it's important to seek professional advice from an employment attorney before you sign any paperwork. Your employer will confirm the deadline for reviewing the offer. The legal requirements for severance can vary depending on the employee's age, whether the termination is isolated or part of a group, and the state where the employee worked.[8]

Jennifer's Story

When Jennifer was fired from her new role, she didn't receive any severance and she was unable to claim unemployment. She had a small emergency fund that would get her through the next three or four months, but that was it.

Jennifer knew she needed to find work fast, but it felt like being fired had blown her career to pieces. She started to wonder if she had what it took to find something new, and she worried about how to explain her sudden departure. All she could think was "Who wants to hire someone who couldn't even do what was needed in their most recent role?"

During her first weeks of unemployment, Jennifer scrolled anxiously through job boards, unsure of where to even start. She was about to start applying for more junior roles when she received a text message from Lisa, a former coworker from her first job. Lisa didn't know that Jennifer was no longer at her new company. She was reaching out to ask if Jennifer could recommend her for a role that had just been posted. It turned out Jennifer's former position was now being advertised.

In that moment Jennifer realized she needed to act. She wrote a brief e-mail to Marcus, her manager at her very first job. Marcus had been sad to see Jennifer leave, and he'd been instrumental in teaching her new skills during her time on his team.

Jennifer didn't sugarcoat her e-mail. She told Marcus she'd been fired and that she didn't know what to do next. Within an hour, Marcus replied, recommending they meet later that week, assuring her that he believed she would find a new role she would thrive in. Jennifer immediately felt her spirits lift a little. Jennifer pulled up her résumé and resolved to update it quickly so she could ask Marcus for his feedback when they met.

"I've Been Furloughed. What Do I Do Now?"

A sudden change of circumstances can be jarring. If you've been furloughed it can be even harder to know how to fill the time you'd usually be working. Creating a new daily routine may require trial and error at first as you figure out what works best for you. While you're in limbo, you're also facing uncertainty about your future and an immediate loss of income. Because you may not be looking for a new role while you wait to hear updates on your current one, you have a different set of needs compared to someone who's lost their job completely.

If you're feeling adrift, my advice is to start with talking to others who have navigated a similar transition. If you don't know anyone personally, ask people in your network if they could connect you with people you know who have been furloughed.

Find ways to stay connected with your coworkers, either as a group or one on one. Do what you can to stay in touch with people in your industry. You may find it comforting to talk about work-related topics during this in-between stage.

You can also use the time to dive into a professional development area you couldn't commit to previously due to your work schedule. That could be taking a course, or pursuing an accreditation, or learning more about a skillset you want to acquire. You may decide you want to share your existing skills and experience with others as a volunteer or mentor. Think about your personal brand, as your furlough period is a great time to update your résumé, gather items for your portfolio if you have one, or update or create a personal website.

If you're worried about your furlough evolving into a layoff, make contingency plans based on three scenarios:

1. Your furlough being extended
2. Layoffs being announced
3. Returning to your role

Using the prompts in this chapter, brainstorm and then jot down the immediate next steps for all three scenarios. A brief contingency plan can make you feel like you have options available for all possible outcomes. Deciding on the actions you would take, if you need to, helps you regain an element of control.

"I've Lost My Job. What Happens Now?" ▬

Before you kick-start your job search in earnest, I want you to commit to three important principles:

1. Process Your Emotions

   Give yourself time and space to work through your feelings. Processing your emotions is tough. It can be upsetting, devastating, and scary. If you're angry, think before you act. Don't say or do something you may regret while your emotions are running high. Don't burn bridges while you're upset. Talk to someone who's been through it. Give yourself space to mourn what happened, get real about your fears, then think about small steps you can take to combat them.

   As a career coach, I advise clients who are working through this to let go of any shame. Almost everyone loses a job at some point in their career. But it will sting. The work we do often has an impact on our identity. It feeds into our self-esteem and fuels our self-confidence. But, when that happens, remember you are much more than a job title. Determine what you can learn from the experience and focus on what you can do next. This is a temporary setback and it won't define you forever. Five years from now you'll look back on what happened with a different perspective. Career changes happen all the time. This won't take away the pain, but soon it will hurt less if you take positive action.

   You're likely to find your emotions will go up and down during the time you're in between roles. That's going to happen. Unknowns are scary and when you're not sure what the future holds, there's a greater chance of obsessing over what's gone wrong. Replaying nightmare scenarios over and over won't help. If you're scared and overwhelmed, try to take things one step at a time and stay focused on asking yourself, "What's the next positive action I can take to help move forward?"

2. Keep Track of Your Finances

Your deadline for landing your next role is likely to hinge on your financial circumstances. When circumstances change suddenly, for almost everyone the first concern is, "How will I cover all of my expenses?"

Figuring out your finances while you look for a job is critical, whether that's an emergency fund, severance, unemployment benefits, or with the support of someone else's income. Don't stick your head in the sand. Create a budget based on what you have and make a commitment to reassess your situation at regular intervals by keeping track of your finances. There are a number of great online tools and apps that can help with this.

3. Make Space for Self-Care

Be kind to yourself as you navigate this process. Losing a job is one of the most stressful life experiences to work through. Prioritizing sleep and regular exercise will unlock the mindset-boosting power of endorphins. Make time in your schedule to take a break and do activities you enjoy. Take time out even if you have job search tasks to complete. Your to-do list will keep going, and self-care isn't a reward for completing tasks—it's essential.

If you feel like you're struggling, seek professional support. A licensed therapist can work with you to help address the challenges you're facing and find ways to help you cope and improve your well-being. If you need help finding resources, talk to a health care provider for advice. Seek help right away if you have difficulty sleeping, feel depressed, or have increased alcohol or other substance use. Make your well-being a priority.

When you've committed to honoring those three things, you'll have a stronger foundation to kick off your job search. Are you ready? Okay, let's get to work.

Decide What You Want

Before you jump headfirst into job boards and applications, I'd like you to start by reassessing your career values carefully and thoughtfully. Don't put a ceiling on your goals just because of your current situation. You can use the Know Your Worth principles in chapter 1 to help cement your career values, create goals, and stay on track with your next steps. If you're considering a career pivot, chapter 7 has recommendations on how to pull off a career change.

When you've decided what you want, create a list detailing the type of roles you're looking for and the type of sectors and companies you are drawn to.

Then create a list of the next steps you need to take, along with the actions needed to help push forward. Spend time brainstorming areas you may need help with or may need to devote time to thinking through in more detail. It's not always possible to figure everything out by yourself. There may be resources, people, or organizations you can tap for help when you know what you want to explore. Keep a list of ideas and actions that people in your network have suggested to you.

Create a Small Support Squad

In addition to connecting broadly with your network, I recommend making a separate, specific ask to a smaller set of people. Ask a few friends if they can be your job search support squad. They will be the people you can talk to about applications submitted, or vent to after a painful phone interview. This provides a safe and encouraging space for you to share each step. A support squad can also help pick you up during tough times and keep you accountable and on track with next steps.

Stay on Top of Next Steps

Job hunting can feel exhausting simply due to the energy and time spent searching for opportunities, racing to complete cover letters and applications, and preparing for interviews.

Sometimes it may feel like you're getting nowhere fast. Try not to get disheartened, because actions build momentum, even if you don't see it or feel it for a while.

Staying on top of next steps, literally one step at a time, will help you stay sane while you're playing the waiting game.

If you're looking for ideas on what your next steps could include, jump ahead to the Dream Bigger Career Toolkit in chapter 9. There you'll find worksheets you can use to shape ideas, actions, and connections you can leverage. Continue to brainstorm new ideas at regular intervals and keep asking others for ideas too.

Scrolling job boards 24/7 won't be healthy for you in the long run. Assign a designated amount of time for job searching and then stop and switch gears. Go to events, listen to podcasts, or read books. These are just a few things that can help spark ideas in between searching for roles.

Ask for What You Need

Tell everyone. Let people know you're looking for work. Don't be shy. People won't be able to help, make suggestions, make introductions, or share opportunities if they don't know.

If you're not sure how to ask, here's an approach you can use:

> **"I'm looking for a new role and would appreciate your support. Ideally, I'm looking for _____. Thank you in advance for any connections, advice, or opportunities you can offer."**

Be specific in your ask and remember that you can tailor what you share with different audiences too. Send messages to former colleagues. Reach out to people you went to school with. Talk to old teachers and bosses. Talk to people in your industry and people who've navigated a similar experience. Ask for a call or a one-to-one catch up. Be clear on what you're looking for.

Look over the actions and next steps lists you created and get help where needed. Don't be afraid to ask, and make it specific. Need someone to help elevate your résumé? Ask the person with the polished LinkedIn profile you admire to lend a hand. Can't find the right roles to apply for? Ask the person with tons of connections if they can introduce you to people on your "I want to work there" list. Need help figuring out answers to the toughest interview questions? Ask someone who recently landed a new role how they prepped.

I recognize this step might feel hard. Depending on your personality, and how you feel about your circumstances, you might not know how to even start a conversation or ask for favors. If this resonates with you, I encourage you to put any fears or doubt aside, just in this instance, because there's power in numbers. The more people who know what you're looking for, the more help you can get.

Find the courage to do what's best for you. Don't worry about judgment. Drop your ego. Tell people. Ask for help.

Remember, most people instinctively like to help others if they can. People don't need to know the details of how you lost your job. They just need to know what you're looking for. The future is the most important part, not what happened in the past.

Don't isolate yourself. You don't have to go it alone just because your last role ended abruptly. Lean on your network for support, connections, and recommendations in the exact same way you would if you were looking for a new role on your own terms. Say yes to every meeting opportunity you can. You may not know the extent of the contacts that person has, and they may be able to connect you with someone else.

Ask for advice but keep in mind that not all advice is equal. You can receive it, but you don't have to apply anyone and everyone's advice. Opinions are subjective. You may hear good ideas and bad ones, you may be sent a connection that leads nowhere, or you may uncover a lead to an amazing opportunity. There's no way of knowing what you may uncover or find helpful, but putting yourself out there is the best way to start.

Revamp Your Résumé

Depending on how long it's been since you were last on the job market, your résumé may need a facelift or a complete overhaul. Working on your résumé is often challenging as it's hard to know when you've got it right. It's also hard to be objective about it because it's centered on your skills and your work.

If you're looking to elevate or completely revamp your résumé, head to the Dream Bigger Career Toolkit in chapter 9. There you will find a checklist to help you figure out what might be missing and over 300 action verbs you can use to showcase your expertise and accomplishments. Revising a résumé can feel overwhelming, especially if it's been a while. Break tasks down into chunks and know each version will get better and better.

The most important thing to remember is to be honest. You don't want to mislead a prospective employer. If you were fired from your most recent role, don't omit the role from your résumé, as tempting as it may be to do so. If a prospective employer uncovers that you lied about your employment history, that will reflect badly on you.

The smartest thing you can do to help mitigate an abrupt end to your most recent role is to prepare a list of stellar references. Think about references before you need them. Create a list of people you'd like to have on standby and ask in advance. Reaching out early has a double advantage, as the people you've shortlisted may also have ideas or contacts to help with your job search.

Jennifer's Story ━━━━━━━━━━━━━━

After meeting with Marcus, her former manager at her very first job, Jennifer started to feel better. She had been afraid that Marcus would see her as a failure, but he was supportive and encouraging when they connected. He told her he would keep her front of mind for any openings and immediately introduced her to two contacts in his network that he thought might be helpful.

Jennifer realized she needed to talk to more people she knew to help broaden her job search options. When she was first fired, she'd just wanted to hide. Now, she realized she needed to act. She started practicing how to explain what she was looking for next and began to send e-mails to former college friends and people she'd connected with during her previous job search.

Jennifer gradually grew more comfortable with asking for what she needed, and she also offered help in return. Jennifer didn't know how long it would take to land her next offer, but she knew she was doing what was needed to push things forward. She embraced the introductions and suggestions she received and focused on preparing for her first interview request.

Conquer Your Interview Nerves

If you're feeling nervous about an interview, take a breath and remember this: You've been called to interview because you are a compelling candidate.

Prepare your "so, tell me about yourself" response and practice sharing at least three examples that convey your relevant experience, skills, and accomplishments.

If you're anxious about how to explain your departure from your previous role, don't be. Preparing and practicing your narrative in advance of your next interview will help build your confidence.

If you were fired, you can use the departure language you agreed to with your previous employer. The most important thing is to not mislead a prospective employer. Be confident, keep it concise, and end your explanation on a positive note.

When asked, "Why did you leave your most recent role?" this is my advice:

- Explain why you're no longer in the role.
- Provide a positive reflection.
- Cement your expertise and what you're looking for now.

For example:

> **"The requirements of my last role didn't align with my strengths. It wasn't the right fit, but it was a valuable learning experience and I appreciate the opportunity I had to do _____. Now I'm excited to pursue roles that are better suited to my skills in _____."**

It's equally important to be prepared for follow-up questions about what led to the firing. If you are asked about it, here's an approach you can take:

- Provide a brief overview of what happened, drawing on your departure language. Don't pass blame or disparage your previous employer.
- Explain concisely what you learned, emphasizing objectivity and professionalism.
- Outline what you now do differently, emphasizing growth and professional development.
- Emphasize some exemplary references; provide names your employer can talk to about your work and accomplishments.

If you were laid off, again, you should feel comfortable with briefly explaining why. Express the reality of the situation, share a key accomplishment during your employment, and emphasize what you're excited to do next.

Here's an example of how to explain that your role was eliminated:

> **"My position was eliminated after our company's revenue dropped substantially. During my time managing the team I was responsible**

for delivering _____. Being let go was unfortunate, but now I'm excited to pursue roles where I can leverage my experience in _____."

Remember, it's likely that the person interviewing you was also in between roles at some point. They may have more empathy than you realize.

Rebounding from Rejection

Rejection is hard, whether it's losing out on a role you've interviewed for or not progressing past the application stage. If you feel like you're getting nowhere fast, or perhaps you've gotten to the final round of interviewing, only to hear a "no thanks," don't give up.

Just because someone says no, or a role evaporates, don't allow it to erode your self-esteem. Who you are, what you do best, and what you need from a role may not align with every opportunity uncovered. Finding the right role takes time.

Don't let other people's actions, or inactions, derail you. Your purpose and your actions supersede everything. Don't give up on yourself, even when you're knocked down. Some people will be able to help you build your career, and some people won't. Some opportunities will help you build your career, and some won't. All experiences are valuable, so if you're interviewing but not getting offers, take what you're learning from the interview process and apply it to the next opportunity.

Remember, rejections mean you're putting yourself out there. That's a good thing. Every "no" or lack of response gets you closer to a "yes." If opportunities seem scarce, it doesn't mean you are not capable of doing the roles you want. It means that the supply is greater than the demand. When this happens, it's harder to find roles and competition is greater. As a result, you may need to temporarily broaden your search if you need to find work fast. This doesn't mean you should give up on searching for your ideal roles. Your career is a journey, and if you must sidestep in the short term because of necessity, that's okay and it doesn't mean you can't get back on track.

Keep going and keep adding new avenues or strategies to try. This is where a support team comes in because it's likely you will need encouragement as well as new ideas and suggestions. Not every idea will be right for you, but there's power in having a team of people looking out for you and suggesting opportunities or making connections, or helping you get creative.

Try to avoid the temptation to compare yourself to others negatively. If you're struggling to lift yourself up, remember all the things you've accomplished and times when you've overcome challenges in the past. Create a list of "triumph over adversity" moments from your own life experiences, from people you know personally and from people you admire. Look at that list when you need a reminder of what you are capable of, and what others have overcome too.

Believe you will bounce back. Everything you experience during your career—the good and the bad—is what makes you stronger. Your next opportunity is just around the corner, so don't give up and don't underestimate your worth in the marketplace. Business is business, jobs come and go, but your career is entirely yours.

You are not the first person to lose your job and you won't be the last. It will not define you forever. Commit to making a fresh start. Your career is for you to define; no one else can do that. Focus on the future; look forward and not back. Soon, you're likely to be amazed at what lies ahead.

Q&A

Here are some questions I've received from people who were bouncing back from a job loss.

I was laid off from my last role and I'm desperate to find my next job. If I get an offer, have I automatically lost my salary negotiation power because I'm unemployed?

> While your prospective employer will be aware you're unemployed right now, that doesn't mean you've lost the power to negotiate a salary offer. Anchor your decision on your needs versus fears of how a negotiation will be perceived. When a prospective employer extends an offer, they want you. Salary negotiation is an expected part of the recruitment process, so review any offers based on your needs and don't be afraid to ask.

I was fired from my last role, and I'm nervous about background checks. What will happen if a prospective employer asks my previous employer about me?

> If you haven't done so already, reach out to your previous employer to determine and agree upon your departure language. If you have been honest with a prospective employer about why you departed from your previous role, there won't be a surprise. If you're in the final round of an interview, you are a strong candidate.

My pay has been cut and I've been furloughed by my employer. I want to look for something new, but I'm worried my reduced salary will affect what I can expect to earn in my next role. What should I do?

> If you are considering new opportunities within a sector that is experiencing contraction, layoffs, or declining revenues,

it's important to be aware that this can have an impact on salary expectations across the board. However, being aware of the broader economic considerations doesn't mean that you are destined to maintain a declining salary. Depending on where you live, it may be illegal for a prospective employer to ask you what you currently earn. I encourage you to focus on your career values, understanding what matters most to you in your next role. If earning over a certain threshold is on that list, own that intention and explore how you can move closer to what you're looking for.

CHAPTER
3

Landing the Salary You Deserve

Money matters, more than ever before. As a career coach, I often work with professionals who are poised to receive fantastic job offers but petrified about negotiating their salaries.

Here's the deal. As a result of the gender pay gap, women of color are chronically underpaid. It has an impact on all of us, even prominent figures. During a panel at the Sundance Film Festival, the Academy Award–winning actress Octavia Spencer shared how she turned to basketball star LeBron James to help negotiate her salary.

IndieWire, an entertainment news site, quoted Spencer as stating, "I think my goal is to make sure that all women of color get equal pay, and all women get equal pay. The only way to do it is to have these conversations, to talk numbers with your co-stars." Spencer recounted how James, an executive producer on the *Madam C.J. Walker* Netflix series she was starring in, became her advocate: "I have to say, when I was negotiating my deal for *Madam C.J.*, LeBron James had to intervene."[1]

When you're interviewing for a new role, you may not have an influential person ready to advocate on your behalf. But don't let that deter you from negotiating, because if you don't ask, you will not get. According to a report published by Randstad, a leading staffing firm, 57 percent of women surveyed had never negotiated their salary.[2]

Today, women and men compete for the same jobs, yet women's earnings still lag those of men at every education level. Research conducted by the Georgetown University Center on Education and the Workforce found the gender wage gap for college graduates increases with age, peaking in their early 50s. Over the course of an entire career, the gender wage gap for workers with bachelor's degrees adds up to more than $1 million. For graduate degree holders, the lifetime earnings differential between men and women is more than $1.6 million.[3]

Let that sink in for a moment. The gender pay gap can make a seven-figure difference to your earning potential, across the course of your career. This is terrifying. The wage gap persists even for women who get more education than men do, even before their careers might be interrupted by parenthood. And, in every major occupational group, men earn more than women.[4]

For underrepresented women, failure to negotiate pay is even more critical. Women of all races are affected by the gender wage gap, although not all women are affected equally. Women consistently earn less than white men, but the differences vary by race and ethnicity. On average, white and Asian American women earn more than Black women, who, in turn, earn more than Hispanic women.

Prior to the onset of COVID-19, the World Economic Forum predicted it would take over 100 years to close the global gender pay gap. Not only does the wage gap widen through the course of women's careers, but it's also strikingly worse for women of color. Research undertaken by the Institute for Women's Policy Research projected it will take until 2130 for Black women to achieve equal pay and Hispanic women will have to wait until 2224.[5] Within a detailed report on gender pay inequity, the Center for American Progress emphasizes the wage gaps for each group are calculated based on median earnings data from the US Census Bureau.[6] As a result, the policy institute reminds readers that the figures do not necessarily represent each individual woman's personal experience.

The data are depressing. Especially when you acknowledge that the wage gaps are just one manifestation of the challenges we face in the workplace as the result of gender, racial, and ethnic bias. When you receive a job offer, you should always negotiate. This chapter will arm you with the approach and insights you need to ask for what you deserve.

Tackling Self-Doubt

When you're starting out, you may feel pressure to accept the first job offer that will kick-start your career. When you're stuck in a job you hate, you may feel pressure to move on the next opportunity as fast as humanly possible. When you're desperate to progress, you may feel pressure to take the job that provides the title, even if the money isn't close to what it should be.

Regardless of your circumstances, what you earn matters at every step in your career, even if it feels like the odds may be stacked against you. Almost everyone experiences imposter syndrome at some point at work. As detailed in chapter 1, imposter syndrome can manifest as feelings of inadequacy that persist despite evident success, in the form of self-doubt and leading you to devalue your worth. It's ironic that these feelings often show up as we're experiencing a career peak, like landing a new role.

Don't let imposter syndrome get in your way during the salary negotiation process. Remember, someone wants to hire you. That's beyond fantastic. If you're nervous about discussing dollars, channel that energy to boost your conviction. This is your moment to determine if the opportunity aligns with your career goals and to make sure the money works too.

Talking about money can feel extremely uncomfortable, but that discomfort does not mean you can sidestep it, because it's so important. The way to move forward is to face any fears you have about asking for what you want. This chapter walks you through the steps you can take to have a conversation about your compensation with confidence.

Recruiters Can Be Anxious Too

Searching for jobs, completing applications, prepping for interviews, and waiting for feedback are some of the most stressful experiences we face as we navigate our careers. This process is unavoidable, it's anxiety-ridden, and the stakes, coupled with our emotions, are usually running high.

As we move through this state of uncertainty, remember it's also challenging for the hiring manager sitting on the opposite side of the interview table. If you've been responsible for filling a position on a team, you'll understand just how hard it can be to find the perfect candidate. In addition, the hiring process is stressful, time-consuming, and expensive.

Did you know?
- According to a study by global staffing firm Robert Half, 70 percent of managers expect candidates to negotiate salary.[7]

- The average cost-per-hire is $4,129, according to data compiled by the Society for Human Resource Management.[8]
- The average time it takes to fill a given position is 42 days.[9]

Due to the time and resources required to recruit the right candidate, hiring managers will often endeavor to gauge salary expectations before an offer is extended. This approach is made to ensure that the expectations of their top candidates align with the salary the role provides.

The factors that affect compensation from a recruiter's perspective include the status of the current job market and demand within the sector; seniority of the role; location; and required qualifications, experience, skills, and responsibilities. The compensation philosophy of the organization will underpin how salary bands are ultimately decided. An employer can choose to lead, lag behind, or match the market when it comes to determining salaries.

Remember, most recruiters fully expect candidates to negotiate their compensation. So, the ball's in your court to decide what you're shooting for.

Preparing for the Money Talk

The first thing you need to do is decide the salary you're targeting at your next role. To do this, you will create a set of three figures.

1. Your Sweet Spot Number.
2. Your Target Salary Range.
3. Your Walk Away Point.

Your Sweet Spot Number is the salary that makes you instinctively smile if you think of it. You won't disclose this magic number during the application and interview process; it's your secret to keep.

Your Target Salary Range represents the set of numbers you would feel comfortable sharing with a prospective employer. The purpose of the Target Salary Range is to get you as close as possible to your Sweet Spot number.

Your Walk Away Point is the lowest salary you would be happy to accept and where you officially draw the line. You won't disclose this threshold to a recruiter, but if you end up with an offer that falls short of this number, you've determined the opportunity is a nonstarter.

As you read this, you may be thinking "Oh, I know exactly what I want to make and what my Walk Away Point is." Alternatively, you might be completely unsure of what to aim for, and where to draw the line. Even if you have instinctive answers for all three figures, you should back up your numbers up with data and research.

Here's how to do it.

Research Salary Brackets

At the start of your job search, before you begin the application process, you should determine the Target Salary Range you are aiming for, as this will help you get closer to your Sweet Spot Number.

Research the salaries for job titles that align with the role you're targeting, and where possible, research salaries for similar roles in the same location as the position you're interviewing for.

Here are some useful salary research resources you can use:

- PayScale
- Salary.com
- Glassdoor
- Indeed
- LinkedIn

- US Department of Labor, Bureau of Labor Statistics
- Publications for your industry
- Professional associations for your industry
- Recruitment agency salary reports for your sector

The online tools allow you to filter compensation searches by a variety of factors including

- Job title
- Location
- Level of education
- Years of experience
- Skills
- Responsibilities
- Number of direct reports

If you're a candidate using salary research tools, you are likely to find a broad array of figures, and it may be hard to determine exactly which numbers to use. Some online tools will provide an estimated pay range. Other tools offer a specific figure based on the data you share and the data they've collated.

Review as many resources as possible, but be prepared to uncover ranges that vary significantly. To help navigate this, be mindful of the size and revenue of the company you are interviewing with. A 50-person firm with a seven-figure balance sheet will have a significantly different pay structure than a 5,000-person firm with billions of dollars in revenue. In addition, consider your level of experience related to the respective role you're targeting. This will affect where you fall within the designated salary band already earmarked by your prospective employer.

Some companies and industry sectors have a degree of salary transparency when it comes to salary bands. Some firms, such as Buffer, a social media management platform, advocate complete salary transparency. The entire team's salaries—from the CEO to marketers—are shared publicly via the company website.[10] Certain companies have gone as far as banning salary negotiations altogether. Reddit, a social news aggregator, made headlines in April 2015 when the company announced it would prohibit salary negotiations for both candidates and existing employees, to close the gender pay gap.

Even if a company keeps their salary bands confidential, hiring managers will research and benchmark salary data for open roles. Dependent on the tools they use, they have the option to purchase a deeper index of statistics that allow companies to filter salary data by additional factors, such as revenue size and number of employees.

If you can, run the salary ranges you've found past someone more senior who works in your industry, to get their perspective. Create a file to save all the data you find, as you may need to refer to it during the interview process. After you've completed your research, you will take the next step to determine the salary you're aiming for.

Decide on Your Sweet Spot

When I'm working with an individual who has researched salaries, often I'll hear, "I've pulled lots of numbers, but I still don't know how what my target salary should be. What do I do?"

Truthfully, there isn't a perfect, failproof technique for finding your sweet spot. Research is essential, but ultimately your sweet spot is yours to determine. One approach you can take is to review your budget and determine your financial needs. Then, when you know how much money you need to earn each year to maintain your lifestyle, ask yourself the following questions:

1. Out of the salary research I've completed, what's the lowest figure I've seen? What's the median and what's the highest?

2. Based on my current circumstances, what's the salary that will comfortably support my financial needs?
3. Based on my current circumstances and the salary research I've conducted, what's a realistic salary that would make me smile?

Your answer to question number three will be your Sweet Spot Number.

It may feel weird landing on your magic number. Do it regardless. And remember, as your career progresses that number will change. Nothing is set in stone forever. Then, when you've decided on your Sweet Spot Number, the goal is to ask for more. Yes, I'd like you to raise the bar higher. Asking for more than the number that makes you smile allows more room for negotiation. This is why you'll create a Target Salary Range.

Land on Your Target Salary Range

To do this, use your Sweet Spot Number as the start of your Target Salary Range. Then, you will consider your level of experience and expertise to create the end number for your range.

I'm in favor of a recommendation made by the American Association of University Women (AAUW) on how to determine the breadth of your range. Officially founded in 1881, AAUW is a nonprofit organization that advances equity for women and girls through advocacy, education, and research. The organization advises early to mid-career professionals to use a 10–15 percent salary range, and up to a 20 percent range for more senior professionals.[11]

I love this recommendation, because the salaries you often find using reports and online tools can present you with ranges that extend by $30,000 or more. If you're a senior leader with a six-, seven-, or eight-figure compensation history, the salary range you land on will be broad, as your compensation packages will be more complex. On the other hand, if you're at the start of your career, or mid-career, the data you find should be refined to the opportunity you're targeting, and your level of experience and skills.

Make sure you can support your Target Salary Range by providing the source of your data if asked. Your Sweet Spot Number, however, should not be shared with a prospective employer. If you're asked about salary expectations, it's always best to deflect until you have an offer. Sometimes that's not possible, and if you're pushed to share your expectations, this is when you'll share your range. It's advantageous to get comfortable with discussing your range and deciding in advance where you can or can't be flexible. To prepare for your negotiation, it's time to decide what you consider to be a dealbreaker.

Determine Your Walk Away Point

Understanding your worth also means that it's important to know your Walk Away Point. This is the lowest salary you would be happy to accept and privately draw the line there. Like your Sweet Spot Number, this is for you alone to know. Don't share this with a prospective employer because it's in your best interests to negotiate for more.

In practice, this may feel hard to do, especially if the stakes are high. Be true to yourself and what you deserve. If it's meant to be, it will be. If it's not right, it's okay to walk away.

How Zahra Bounced Back from a Big Mistake

It took 77 applications and over two dozen interviews before Zahra finally found her first job as a junior front-end developer. She hadn't intended to keep count of her strikeout rate, but as time progressed, she figured the odds would eventually fall in her favor. It was hard, but she kept scrolling job boards for openings, and tweaking and sending out résumé after résumé.

Eventually a first interview turned into a second interview, which resulted in an unexpected job offer. Zahra promptly burst into tears after the call with HR. It had taken so much to get to that point that Zahra didn't even consider negotiating salary. This was her first job offer and it had taken so long to secure it.

But, after 18 months in her role, Zahra was ready to move on and this time she intended to clarify what to ask for. Zahra decided she wanted to translate the skills she'd accumulated to work on bigger projects. She had recently attended a workshop for women in tech that shared a list of online salary tools. After an hour on her laptop, Zahra was speechless. Her screen showed salaries ranging from $47,000 all the way to $65,000. For the past six months, Zahra had been struggling to cover her rent, tuition fees, and expenses with her salary. Based on her budget, she decided her Sweet Spot Number for a new role was $50,000 and her Walk Away Point was $46,000.

After talking to a senior front-end developer, Zahra decided her Target Salary Range would be $50,000–$55,000. Doing the research in advance felt like a game-changer. Coupled with her work experience and portfolio, Zahra now knew exactly what to look for, and ask for, in her next role.

Select Your Pay Me More Proof Points

As discussed in chapter 1, keeping track of your accomplishments is essential. They are vital for when it comes to preparing what I like to call Pay Me More Proof Points. Prepping a short, impressive list of accomplishments will emphasize the qualifications, proven skills, and specific achievements that prove your worth to your next employer.

Consider your biggest career achievements to date and write them down. You can use the most compelling proof points as part of your salary negotiation script. Yes, if you've received an offer to join their team, your next employer is aware of your abilities. However, it's affirming to underscore your biggest wins and strongest skills during a salary negotiation.

Get Ready to Be Asked About Salary Expectations

At some point, whether it's within a job application form, or during an interview, you are likely to be asked about your salary expectations. It's smart to be prepared.

As a first step, it's important to know your rights, as labor and employment laws are constantly changing. At the time of writing this book, in several states in the United States, including California, Massachusetts, and New York, it's illegal for prospective employers to ask about your salary history. Take time to research the regulations in the employer's state when you start the application process. If an interviewer is breaking the law, that's a huge red flag.

If you're asked about salary expectations as part of an online application, here are your options:

- If the application field allows a text response write in "negotiable."
- If the form requires numerals and the field is mandatory, put your Target Salary range based on your search (only if you absolutely must).
- If the form field won't allow you to enter a range and insists on just one number, then use the median figure from your Target Salary Range. Only do this if the form field is mandatory.

If you're asked about salary expectations during an interview, do whatever you can to deflect. Here are some ways you can sidestep the ask:

- "I'd like to learn more about the role before discussing salary expectations."
- "I'm confident the role will have a salary that reflects the market rate for the skills and expertise required."

If your interviewer is persistent and won't let you sidestep the question, this is where you share your Target Salary Range. This is one of the major reasons why I recommend researching and considering salary in advance so if you're pushed to do so, you only share what you'd happily accept.

When the time comes to talk about money, I always advocate sharing your Target Salary Range versus your salary history with a prospective employer. Your salary history should not have an impact on the salary of your next role. Of course, what you've earned previously will matter to you, and it will likely fuel your drive to keep progressing. However, salary history can hold you back when it comes to advancing your earning potential. As I discussed at the start of the chapter, the gender pay gap is deeply entrenched and it reaches every industry, across every sector. Salary history questions can disproportionately affect women by perpetuating pay inequities. Don't divulge how you've been paid in the past; instead, focus your next employer's attention on what you expect to earn.

Negotiate Your Job Offer

If you've received a job offer, first things first: Congratulations! If you need it, ask for time to review the offer in writing. Check with the recruiter how much time they can provide, and make sure to meet the deadline.

Then, if you've decided you'd like to accept the offer, it's time to negotiate.

My advice is to negotiate only if you really want the role. If you're not excited about the opportunity, assess the reasons why by reviewing your career values and getting clear on those first, before you begin the negotiation process. If you're negotiating, you should be serious about accepting an offer from the company because it's more than likely they will make a concession to move closer to your ask.

Employers will rarely start with a best offer. That's how most organizations operate, as they want the best people for the best price. In essence, there are three possible outcomes to a salary negotiation:

1. The employer says no and refuses to negotiate.
2. The employer increases their offer to move it closer to your ask.
3. The employer meets or exceeds your request.

Know what matters most to you. Complete the career values exercise in chapter 1 before you start the salary conversation, as this will help you assess how the role aligns with your goals.

Compensation package components can include:

- Base salary
- Benefits, for example health insurance, dental insurance, vision insurance, retirement plans, life insurance, paid time off
- Overtime
- Commission
- Stock options
- Profit sharing
- Signing bonus

- Performance bonuses
- Additional perks, such as flexible work schedules, paid parental leave, commuter benefits, employee discounts, parking stipends, relocation packages, phone allowance, fitness memberships, or professional development resources

I always recommend asking potential employers about professional development opportunities. Some companies allocate each employee a specific budget for coaching, courses, or specific training the individual has chosen to pursue.

Consider everything within the offer and decide what matters most to close the deal. If salary and something else, such as the allocation of paid time off, are issues, address both at the same time. You want to avoid a scenario where you negotiate a higher salary, get it, and then go back to the recruiter to ask for more paid time off. Decide at the outset what matters most, and in this case if the money and vacation time are both top of your list, negotiate both at the same time, not sequentially.

The more senior you are, the more complex your compensation package will be, and this in turn is likely to provide more depth for negotiations. Decide which benefits matter the most to you as you review the offer. If something essential is missing, assess if it would be a dealbreaker.

There might be less flexibility to negotiation components of a health insurance package or 401K package, as employers are usually part of a plan, but there can be wiggle room in other areas, such as paid time off or relocation assistance.

Make the Ask

Before you make the ask, adopt a positive mindset. At every stage of the negotiation process, be engaged, enthusiastic, and a good listener. Money matters, but you also want to convey to your next employer that you're excited about the new opportunity. I always recommend that candidates negotiate directly in conversation, versus over e-mail. When the opportunity presents itself, where possible ask for a direct conversation.

Here's an approach you can use to start the negotiation:

Part One: Start with a thank you and convey excitement about the opportunity.

Part Two: Share a compliment. This should be specific to your interview process, the team, or the company.

Part Three: Explain that you need to discuss compensation.

Part Four: Share your first Pay Me More Proof Point.

Part Five: Share your Target Salary Range.

Part Six: Close by reiterating your excitement about the opportunity and ask if you can continue the conversation.

Here's an example of how this approach could sound:

Part One:

"Thank you for sharing the offer details for the financial analyst position. I'm elated about the opportunity to join the company."

Part Two:

"I enjoyed meeting the leadership team last week, and I appreciate the time you allocated to show me the office."

Part Three:

"Before I can accept your offer, I'd like to discuss the proposed compensation."

Part Four:

"As I shared with the team director, in my current role I maintained and monitored the performance analysis and record maintenance for our business unit, reducing material costs by 15 percent in one year."

Part Five:

"Given my areas of expertise, I'm seeking a salary in the range of $75,000 to $82,000, which is slightly higher than your offer of $70,000."

Part Six:

"I'd love to join your team and use my skills to help accelerate the division's performance. Is it possible to discuss the proposed salary further?"

Be ready to detail the sources for your salary range research, if asked. If there's pushback, you can use your second Pay Me More Proof Point and then reiterate that you hope you can work together to land on a salary that reflects your experience and expertise.

During the negotiation process, remain positive and flexible, and continue to demonstrate how your skills match the employer's needs. Avoid getting personal or oversharing. Keep any nerves or emotions in check. Be reasonable, responsive, and professional from start to finish. If you are evasive, difficult, or unprofessional, a recruiter will walk away. Don't drag out a negotiation. If your respective starting points are too far apart, or you are hoping for a better opportunity, it's a sign this role probably isn't the right one.

Closing the Deal

Waiting for an answer after you've asked for more money can feel excruciating, but remember, you've already done the hardest thing. You've nailed a job interview and you've asked for the salary you want. The rest is up to the person who wants to be your next employer.

When you hear the response, take a moment to gauge how you feel. If you're excited, congratulations! If you're disappointed, you will need to consider quickly if the role is the right one for you.

As we embark on a new chapter in our career, there will always be question marks and uncertainty, but trust the core feeling in your gut. If the company has presented a counteroffer that exceeds your Walk Away Point, your work is done; no further negotiation is needed.

Often our circumstances affect how we review an opportunity, so the decision to say yes or no to an opportunity is a personal one. I will always ask underrepresented women to advocate their worth by negotiating salary.

How Elizabeth Asked for More ━━━━

Every hour, on the hour, Elizabeth checked her inbox, just in case. It had been 36 hours since her final interview for an art director role at an ad agency she'd admired for the longest time. At the end of the meeting, the hiring manager told her they wanted her to join the team. As a next step, she would be in touch within the next business day with a written offer.

After refreshing her inbox over and over, there it was. Elizabeth clicked on the message and quickly scanned it before slumping back in her chair and scrolling slowly through it again. The agency had offered to pay her $4,000 less than she was currently earning. Elizabeth closed her eyes and took a deep breath. She had worked so hard and waited so long for this opportunity. But the pay was so low. She was nervous, but she knew deep down that she needed to act.

A few months prior, Elizabeth had spotted a detailed salary report in the industry magazine her company subscribed to. Based on what she'd learned, Elizabeth knew she needed to be earning $85,000–$102,000 in her next role, and her personal Sweet Spot

Number was $85,000. But right now, the offer in her inbox wasn't close to where she wanted to be.

Elizabeth dug out the notes she'd made as she prepared for the first round of interviews. She wanted to remember the accomplishments she'd shared during the initial conversations, and some of the challenges the creative director had discussed during their first meeting. She opened her e-mail and sent a reply expressing her enthusiasm for the role, but asking if they could connect to review the compensation.

Then, she went back to waiting, feeling even more anxious than before.

This time, instead of an e-mail reply, Elizabeth's cell phone rang within 30 minutes. It was the hiring manager. She thanked Elizabeth for her quick response and asked if they could discuss the offer over the phone. Elizabeth emphasized how much she admired the firm's creative work, highlighted the awards her campaigns had won that year, and emphasized how she could make an immediate impact with their upcoming projects. Elizabeth didn't want to reference her current salary, so she opted to use the salary range she had prepared in advance instead.

The hiring manager listened carefully, before offering to counter Elizabeth's request with a revised offer of $90,000. For a moment, Elizabeth was speechless. She accepted the offer, hung up the phone and sat still in disbelief. She'd done it. She had an offer from a firm she was dying to work for and landed the salary she'd dreamed of.

I want you to have a salary negotiation that results in a happy ending. It can take a long time to find the right role, and when you find the right role, it's equally important to make sure the money is right too. To do that, you must prepare, practice, and persist when it comes to negotiating your salary.

Salary negotiation is a process that's designed to find a compromise that works for both parties—you and your prospective employer. It's not a tug-of-war where one person wins and the other person loses. Your prospective employer wants to hire you and you want to work for the company. Finalizing terms is an important part of the process.

Negotiating your salary allows you to lay a solid foundation for doing your best work in your new role. It also increases your earning potential for your entire lifetime. Lay a solid foundation for doing your best work in your new role and use your negotiation skills as a springboard to your next promotion.

Q&A

Here are some questions I've been asked about negotiating during the job search process.

I want this job so bad, but I'm afraid to ask for more. What do I do next?

If you're offered a job, you're in a fantastic position. Don't feel you'll jinx it by negotiating your salary. The opportunities to cement your worth are often few and far between. Don't let the opportunity to discuss money pass you by just because you're afraid to ask.

The best way to move past fear is by facing it and taking positive action. Trust me, learning to negotiate is a skill that will pay dividends in the long run for your career. Do your research and practice your salary script over and over until you become comfortable making the ask.

Remember, the idea of asking is much scarier than what it will entail. Recruiters fully expect for first offers to be countered. How does the offer compare to what you want? Focusing on next steps will help you move past the fear factor toward negotiating the final terms for a role you can't wait to start.

If feels weird asking for more when people are taking pay cuts or losing their jobs. Can I still negotiate when the economy is bad?

Yes. You can and should still negotiate your salary even during an economic downturn. It's smart to be mindful of the financial performance of your prospective employer and the industry they are in. Do your research to ascertain your Target Salary Range reflects your level of expertise and industry benchmarks. It's also important to consider the economic climate. When there's a shortage of job opportunities and a surplus of potential hires, that can have an impact on the negotiating leverage a candidate may have. These are important considerations but your situation, needs, and career goals are paramount. Only you can determine what you need from your next role. In contrast, if the company is hiring, they have their own needs also. If they have a need and want to hire you, you are fully entitled to negotiate your compensation.

I've been lowballed and they won't budge. What do I do now?

When it comes to difficult decisions, be clear on your priorities and your dealbreakers, and then assess how the opportunity aligns. When you've determined these in advance, it's much easier to make choices regarding next steps.

Review the career priorities exercise detailed in chapter 1 and assess how the opportunity aligns with everything you're looking for. If you completed the exercise prior to receiving the offer, review it again now that you know more about the company and the compensation.

If the salary offered is significantly below the lowest figure on your Target Salary Range, you should share your range. You will also need to understand that this employer may not be able to meet your needs. If they won't increase their offer, of if they increase their offer and it still falls short of your Walk Away Point, you have already created a contingency plan.

Ultimately, the decision is a personal one that only you can make, but trust your gut when it comes to deciding whether to walk away or say yes to less.

I've been approached by a recruitment consultant about a role. How should I approach salary questions from a recruiter?

A recruiter will handle the negotiation between you and the prospective employer, so you should feel comfortable sharing your Target Salary Range with the consultant. Recruiters' fees are usually based off a candidate's first year of income. They are incentivized to advocate for their candidate, because they want to place you in the role, but you still must clarify and communicate your career objectives.

Should I still negotiate if the salary I've been offered is more than I'm currently making?

Yes, you can still negotiate, and you should. The "more" in this statement is key, as the amount offered may signify a small leap or a significant one. Whether the salary offered is a little bit more or a lot more than you're making, the core principle still stands. Employers rarely make their best offer out of the gate. So yes, you can negotiate.

Instead of focusing on the fact that the offer is more than your current salary, I encourage you to assess how the offer compares to your Sweet Spot Number. If the offer is more than that secret number that makes you smile, you're in a fantastic position where you have exceeded your financial goal.

Take time to consider the responsibilities of the new role and what you've learned during the interview process. Business is business, so if you're earning a significant salary, you will fulfill a key role for your new employer. Don't question it. Employers hire employees to leverage their expertise and skills to achieve specific business objectives. If an employee doesn't deliver, the employee loses their job, and the employer will hire someone else. Your salary derives from a specific business need. This is a great position to be in, as you don't have to negotiate as hard. Congratulations on securing an exciting and, I hope, rewarding opportunity.

PART II
PUSH

4

How to Position Yourself for a Promotion

What's the scariest thing you've ever asked for at work? Many years ago, I finally summoned up the courage to ask my boss for a promotion. I had spent four years consistently achieving results. I knew my boss was happy with my work, so I wanted patiently for the reward that never came. Over time, I'd become so discouraged that when my boss cancelled and then forgot to reschedule my performance review, I just shrugged and didn't question it. Six months later, I realized I needed to seize the initiative. If I didn't ask for what I wanted it might never happen. I committed to preparing for the next cycle of performance reviews, and this time I made sure that my meeting didn't slip off the calendar.

When the time came to meet for my performance review, I was quietly terrified, but I did it. I asked for a promotion and I got it. When I finally used my voice my boss confessed that he assumed I was in the promoted role already. He was excited to discuss the future, and we worked together on the next steps to announce my new title.

I'm sharing this story because it underscores what I see time and time again in my work as a coach. Women of color are doing the work and achieving the results that deserve a promotion. But we are not always seen. This chapter will show you how to build a case and make the ask.

If you're eager to take the next step in your career, you need a promotion push strategy. Working hard and waiting for your boss to notice is not enough. The opportunity gap for women of color is real. Most of us don't need to look at data to know just how hard it is to level up. We are already living it. But that's why it's even more important to keep pushing.

So, how do you create a promotion push strategy? Here are 10 steps that will set you up for success:

1. Understand what your target role requires.
2. Create your career growth plan.
3. Be visible.
4. Understand the decision-making process.
5. Align with advocates.
6. Research salary brackets.
7. Create your Promotion Proof Points.
8. Be prepared for pushback.
9. Practice the promotion conversation.
10. Ask for it.

Step 1: Understand What Your Target Role Requires

This first step lays the foundation for everything. If you want to be considered for a promotion, you need to understand what the role requires and be ready to demonstrate where your skills and experience align. Research the requirements for the role you're targeting and be ready to show how you can deliver. Understand what success looks like, based on the goals of your leadership, and then be productive, add value, and deliver results.

Think about how you show up for meetings, whether they are on the phone, video, or in person. Think about what you want to convey and pay attention to your body language. Sitting up straight conveys attentiveness, while slouching in your seat or during a meeting silently screams that you don't want to be there. Smiling and making appropriate eye contact doesn't just build rapport, it also makes you appear trustworthy and confident. Your physical cues are just as important as your verbal ones.

Continue to be consistently professional and positive as you do your work and in your day-to-day interactions. This builds trust in your abilities and personal attributes. Don't overpromise and underdeliver. Do what you'll say you'll do. Be on time. Meet deadlines. When you lead by example, people notice. Leverage the unique skills you bring and play to your strengths. Developing good communication channels with your boss works in your favor in the long run. Be a good listener; embracing feedback and using it to your advantage will help you move ahead. Even if you make a mistake along the way, that's okay. You can move forward by learning from it. Be a good team player. A great way to demonstrate the professionalism needed for leadership is to avoid gossip and treat everyone with respect.

If you consistently and successfully solve problems for your manager, you will stand out. Early in my career I learned an important lesson. Without realizing it, I had the tendency to point out why something wouldn't work. During one of my observations, my manager turned to me and said, "Don't come to me with the problem; come to me with the solution." In that moment, a light bulb went off for me. I thought I was being helpful by pointing out the hurdles. I was wrong. What I needed to do was to identify potential problems and present ideas for how we could avoid them.

Step 2: Create Your Career Growth Plan

Creating a career growth plan will enable you to map out your next steps and take actions to propel you forward. This plan is for your own personal use. It will include the accomplishments, skills, and attributes you need to build for your future roles, including the next step you're looking to make.

Feedback you receive from your manager on the job or in performance reviews is essential. But your career growth plan should extend even further. It will become the blueprint for your future.

Creating a career growth plan may feel a bit overwhelming at first. That's okay. Remember, you don't have to have everything worked out right now. Your career growth plan will evolve over time. It's something you should start, but you will update it over time as you progress and gather more insights.

When you're targeting a promotion, review relevant job descriptions and align your skills. Take time to consider the strengths and traits that support you, as well as the weaknesses and traits that can make you less effective, and how you can address those.

Be as objective as you can and consider feedback you may have received in your performance reviews or from others during your career. Get real about your strengths and weaknesses.

Here's an exercise that can help you dig a little deeper so you can create an action-oriented plan. You can find a blank version of this Career Growth Plan in the Dream Bigger Career Toolkit in chapter 9.

Exercise 1

1. Pick an area or skill you want to develop.
2. Create a list with two columns.
3. On the left-hand side, jot down everything that could be an obstacle to achieving this skill or developing in this area.
4. On the right-hand side, jot down ideas of how you might solve that.

For example, imagine you've been asked to be more visible in client meetings, but the prospect of presenting to a large group makes you panic.

Skill needed: Deliver presentations with confidence at team meetings

Obstacle	Solution
Nerves.	Find opportunities to present to smaller groups.
Limited time to create what would be needed.	Ask if I could partner with someone to prepare the slides.
Unfamiliar with the tech needed.	Schedule time with IT to walk through tech tools.

Look at each component on your career growth plan and assign each item a next step. When you've taken that step, go back to your plan and look at the next item and choose the next step you'll take.

Always ask yourself:

What will I commit to doing next?

Consider the skills you want to learn and what tools and resources are available to do that. Identify whether your employer offers in-house training. You may be surprised to learn what resources are already available for you to use. If your employer doesn't offer the training you need, they may offer to invest in your professional development, so it's always advantageous to discuss your goal. Outside of your company, explore what your industry's associations have to offer; they are likely to have a range of events, courses, and resources you can leverage. Talk to your network for recommendations, too.

Be proactive and show that you're ready to step up. Keep setting goals for your professional development and stay focused on achieving them.

Step 3: Be Visible

Being visible matters because underrepresented candidates are often overlooked. According to a recent study by Working Mother Media, multicultural women are 25 percent more likely to aspire to senior roles than white women. However, our aspirations can fall by the wayside fast. Working Mother Media's research found only 46 percent of multicultural women had attended a meeting with senior executives within a two-year period, compared to 63 percent of white men.[1]

There are two components to this. First, make sure your work and your accomplishments are visible to your manager. Do you have a regular meeting on the calendar? Don't wait until your performance review to share your accomplishments. Share your wins on a regular basis and use your meetings to your advantage. Second, when you have that base covered, you need to consider additional individuals, teams, or leaders who you should engage with at your company to enhance your visibility.

The second part may seem tricky or daunting, especially if you are working remotely or don't have access to the spaces where important conversations take place. Don't be disheartened. Instead, use this exercise to ask yourself the following questions, as your responses will help spark ideas.

Exercise 2

1. What do you want to be known for within your company?
2. What do you need to start doing more of?
3. Who are the decision makers who are pivotal to your advancement?
4. Who are the people at your company that can open doors for you or advocate for you?
5. Who at your company is already a champion of your work?
6. Are there groups, programs, or committees at your company that you could join to broaden your internal networks?
7. What opportunities are there to raise awareness of your work or build relationships with decision makers?
8. What will you commit to doing next?

If you are clear on your intentions, you will be open to opportunities as and when they appear. Consider where you could step up and deliver impact to a business objective that's important to leadership. Don't forget your peers and junior members of the team. Ask your manager if there are areas where you can lend support to help solve a problem by guiding more junior team members. Maybe you could teach someone a new skill or share insights that can help increase productivity. Where possible, ask your manager for stretch assignments that can help add value to the team.

Actions speak louder than words. Do what you can to consistently demonstrate your ability to do the promoted role, even before it's yours.

Lori's Story

Lori had been at her company for four years. She worked hard and consistently received good feedback from her manager. Her company always announced promotions shortly after the start of the new fiscal year. Lori was quietly confident that her loyalty and her track record would be recognized with a promotion. She waited patiently, but a few days before the formal announcements, Lori was stunned to discover one of her coworkers, Damon, had been promoted to lead her team.

Lori and Damon had worked together recently on a project, so when she reached out to congratulate him, she asked if they could grab a coffee to discuss his new role. During that conversation, Lori learned that Damon had approached their manager 18 months previously to ask about the requirements for a promotion, and then applied the advice she had given. He'd started attending monthly executive meetings where he shared updates on their project.

Lori slowly realized she'd been working hard on all the deliverables, but she hadn't taken the steps she needed to be more visible. She decided to follow Damon's lead and made the decision to talk to her manager for the first time about her long-term career goals.

Step 4: Understand the Decision-Making Process

Depending on the size of your company, the decision-making process for promotions can vary substantially. Ask your manager for guidance if you're unclear on any of the steps.

In this exercise are some questions to ask yourself. If you don't know the answers, then it will identify the areas you need to clarify.

Exercise 3

1. What is the criteria for a promotion?
2. Is the promotion process documented?
3. When does the next performance review cycle begin?
4. Does your company provide professional development resources for individuals targeting a promotion?
5. How does leadership measure success?
6. Who are the decision makers?
7. Is there a business case for your promotion?
8. How would my promotion affect the broader team or organization?
9. Is my manager an advocate for my advancement?

After you've completed this self-assessment, identify the areas where you need to dig a little deeper and identify the next steps you need to take. These could include scheduling a one-on-one meeting with your manager. If you have a mentor at your company, you could ask if they have insights or guidance. Alternatively, if there are people at your company who were recently promoted, they might be happy to share how they navigated the process.

If you want to be promoted, it's important to be proactive by laying the foundations as early as possible. Your company is likely to have a certain time frame during the fiscal year when promotion opportunities are considered. Some companies have a set parameter for promotions in terms of skills, qualifications, and experience, so it's important to know the protocols where you work. Based on what you know, create your own promotion time line.

In addition, there are contingent factors that will have an impact on how leadership at your company addresses promotion opportunities. Business cycles and the restructuring of teams—due to reorganizations, mergers, layoffs, or resignations—will affect your career trajectory. Your performance is pivotal, but it's also critical to understand the broader business context. Be aware of what's required to take the next step in terms of your attributes, skills, and achievements as well as the bigger picture needs for your team, department, or organization.

When it comes to what you can control, you need to start a regular dialogue with your manager, using your performance review conversations as a foundation. Working hard and waiting for your boss to notice will not guarantee a promotion. Plant the seed early. Your manager needs to know your goals, and you also need to understand what your manager's goals are for the team, and how you can add value.

Promotions can take a long time to manifest. With that in mind, be ready to play the long game, and build trust with your boss so that when you make the formal ask, if won't be a complete surprise.

Step 5: Align with Advocates

If you want to advance, cultivating relationships with people in leadership roles is crucial. Ideally, your manager should be one of your biggest advocates. Sometimes that's the case; sometimes it's not. If your performance review feedback is consistently positive, but your manager is not an advocate for you or your work, you have two options:

1. Give up. Stop engaging and stop delivering.
2. Keep aiming high regardless. Continue to set new goals and demonstrate your skills, attributes, and accomplishments.

You can't control your manager's actions; however, you can control how you show up for work, what you deliver, and what you choose to do next. Cultivating networks of advocates will help you advance faster.

Here's an exercise to help you move forward.

Exercise 4

1. Create a wish list of potential advocates. Ideally this will include people who are already aware of your skills and attributes.
2. Identify opportunities to share your accomplishments and show your leadership skills to individuals on your wish list.
3. Be clear about your goals and ask for their feedback.

Remember that relationships don't happen overnight and take time to develop. Someone on your wish list may not be receptive. That's okay. You can "raise your hand" but the potential advocate must choose to support you. Ask for their advice and listen to their insights. Feedback is valuable. Use it to keep cultivating your networks and finding avenues to shine.

If you don't have the support of an advocate within your company, the opportunities to advance will be limited. Cement your reputation by continuing to do great work. Remember, sometimes you won't know when people are advocating for you. If you consistently do great work, people around you will notice.

A person who advocates for you may also be a mentor. Mentors aren't always easy to find. Sometimes mentoring is intentional, where companies or organizations endeavor to pair mentors and mentees. Often, mentoring can happen by chance where a relationship develops organically over time.

If your company doesn't provide a formal mentoring program, try to find opportunities to talk to people in the role you want, inside and outside your company, to learn how they got there.

Introductions and first conversations may spark a longer-term mentoring relationship.

The role of a mentor and an advocate can overlap, and the following table shows how to differentiate between the two. You can't control if a mentor, your manager, or a senior leader will become an advocate for you, but when it happens, it's powerful.

MENTOR	ADVOCATE
A senior leader in your company or within your professional network	A senior leader in your company or within your professional network
Shares their own direct insights on how they navigated career milestones and challenges	Amplifies your work to decision makers
Provides advice by sharing their own perspectives or stories	Opens doors by presenting new opportunities and connections for you
Provides perspectives on career choices and strategies	Uses their influence to aid your advancement
Reacts to your questions	Is proactive in pushing you forwards
Tells you what to do	Acts on your behalf

Remember, it's important to always be an advocate for yourself. Maintain your accomplishments list and be ready to talk about your skills and achievements with confidence.

Nicole's Story

Nicole was reeling. She had recently applied for a more senior internal position that she really wanted. Her company was expanding into a new market and was looking for a director to oversee a new business unit. Nicole was beyond excited about the opportunity, until she received the call from the hiring manager to tell her that her application had been unsuccessful.

The hiring manager told Nicole that they needed a candidate with a track record of executing strategies in the new market. Nicole was crushed. In addition to the disappointment, she was worried that she may have burned bridges on her current team by pursuing a new role.

After a chance conversation while on their way to another meeting, Nicole discovered that the managing director of her office was thrilled that she raised her hand for the new opportunity. She gave Nicole additional insights regarding the unique needs the leadership team required for the role and encouraged her to keep doing great work. Nicole realized she had a potential advocate who she could approach about additional opportunities to grow her career.

Step 6: Research Salary Brackets

If you've yearned for a promotion, landing the new title you've dreamed of feels fantastic. In addition, a new title means new responsibilities, and new responsibilities mean more money. My advice is to wait to discuss salary until you have been offered a new role, but it's important to be prepared. Don't skip over researching salaries. You should approach the salary research for your targeted promotion in the same way you would research salaries for a new role at a new company.

As detailed in chapter 3, this means prepping a set of numbers in advance of your promotion conversation. The goal is to land the promotion first and then finalize your compensation package when your new role and responsibilities have been decided.

Unless you work at a company or organization that has salary transparency, it can be hard to research internal salary brackets. In addition, most people aren't comfortable with sharing what they earn. Don't let that derail you. You can leverage salary surveys within your industry that are collated and published by professional associations or recruiters who specialize in your sector. You can also pull numbers using external salary resources, such as PayScale, LinkedIn, and Glassdoor.

Landing on a salary range you are comfortable sharing during the negotiation phase lays the foundation for moving closer to your Sweet Spot Number. Sharing a range also conveys to your employer that you are open to negotiation, by providing space and consideration for the contingent factors that affect your employer's compensation parameters.

As detailed in chapter 3, always consider your career priorities before you start negotiating and determine where salary aligns within those priorities. For example, in addition to a new title, you may also want to negotiate performance bonuses, stock options, PTO, additional benefits, location, or components of the role, in addition to salary.

Step 7: Create Your Promotion Proof Points

Before you ask for a promotion, you will need to build a case and be ready to share it. To get started, you will review your accomplishments and create a list of Promotion Proof Points.

Consider what you've achieved, quantify the results, and emphasize the benefits to your company or team as a result. Using data to back up your achievements is powerful, as metrics clearly demonstrate the value of your contribution to your company. Each Promotion Proof Point should contain these three components:

1. Your accomplishment
2. The results
3. The benefits/value

Here's an example:

Accomplishment

I created a process to document key stages and results for our newest program at every step instead of recapping the project at the end.

Result

I was able to create the first case study within 10 days of the project's completion using my process tracker.

Benefit

The case study was shared with 11 new business leads, which resulted in the acquisition of three new clients.

Prepare as many Promotion Proof Points as you can and then put them in order of importance. You will start with the strongest, and if you need to keep the conversation going, you'll have more examples to expand on.

To do this effectively, you need to track your accomplishments on a regular basis. I advise my coaching clients to do this at the end of each month. I ask them to set a calendar reminder to write down key actions they took and the results. Commit to creating a career accomplishments master file that you update every month or at the very least every quarter.

In addition to sharing the results and benefits of your accomplishments, you should prepare a Promotion Proof Point that looks ahead. Understand the skills required of the role you're targeting. Consider objectives that are important to your team, department, and the broader organization. Be ready to emphasize how you can deliver results in the elevated role.

Here's an example:

> *"In a project manager role, I'd love to leverage my critical thinking and leadership skills to increase productivity for the team so we can best support the department's goals for the next fiscal year."*

It's important to make the business case, not just the personal case, for your promotion using your Promotion Proof Points. Decide which one to lead with, to highlight the value your work adds to the organization. Then, you can also emphasize how your personal attributes will enable you to continue to deliver in the promoted role. Personal factors, such as financial needs or the honest truth that you're tired of waiting, should not be a part of your promotion conversation with your manager. Keep the conversation focused on the business case. Don't compare yourself to others. Your personal finances or your professional time line will not be your boss's primary concern.

Dani's Story

What would she do if her boss said no? Dani didn't know the answer to that question. But she was tired, stressed, and close to the breaking point. She knew if things remained the same, she'd become increasingly resentful. Over the past year, Dani's workload had doubled. She was constantly putting out fires and dealing with complex schedules for a demanding client. Her manager was leaning on Dani more and more and seemed to enjoy passing along some of the toughest assignments with the tightest turnaround times.

For the longest time Dani dealt with it. She didn't complain and she did what was needed. One afternoon, Dani was part of a group chat with a coworker, who achieved far less, when he made the case for why he should be promoted. Dani couldn't believe it. That night she worked late, but instead of tackling her to-do list she decided to do something different. She started drafting an e-mail listing all the things she was responsible for and what she had accomplished. She decided she would schedule time with her manager to talk about her future and ask for a promotion.

Step 8: Be Prepared for Pushback

In advance of your promotion conversation, consider the alternate ways your manager may react and plan your response. In essence, there are three possible outcomes:

1. Your manager supports your request for promotion.
2. Your manager is noncommittal.
3. Your manager turns down your request for promotion.

Outcome 1: Your manager is supportive.

If your manager is supportive of your ask, that's fantastic! You should use the rest of the conversation to learn more about next steps.

Outcome 2: Your manager is noncommittal.

If your manager is noncommittal, use open-ended questions to gather insights or feedback. Be ready to listen carefully to the responses.

If your manager says:

"I can't make any promises right now" or "I have a lot to consider before I can discuss future opportunities."

Your response could be:

> *"That's helpful to know. When would be the best time to revisit the conversation?"* or *"Thank you for the guidance. Could you share some insights on the promotion process and considerations?"*

Outcome 3: Your manager turns down your request.

If your manager turns down your request for promotion, take a deep breath. It will be hard to hear, but where possible, try to put your emotions to one side until the conversation has ended and you have time to process everything.
If your manager says:

> *"We're not considering promotions at this time"* or *"You're not ready to make that transition yet."*

Your response could be:

> "I'd really value your insights and advice. Can you guide me on the skills or experience I'd need to make the next step in my career?" or "Thank you for the feedback. What does the promotion process look like, and do you have any advice for me?"

If you take time in advance to think through how you would respond to pushback, you will be prepared for every possible scenario.

Step 9: Practice the Promotion Conversation

So, you've done the work, prepped your success statements, and crunched your numbers. Now it's time to practice making the ask.

1. **Start the conversation with a compliment.**
2. **Convey what you love about your role.**
3. **Share your Promotion Proof Point.**
4. **Make your ask.**

Reiterate what excites you about the opportunity to advance at the company.

Here's an example of how this could sound:

> *"Thank you for advocating for our team to lead the end-of-quarter presentations. That was a fantastic opportunity for us. I'm incredibly proud to have created the systems our team has used to improve productivity and sales and hit our KPIs for the past four quarters in a row. I've been thinking about how I can continue to add value to our department as we plan for the new fiscal year. My goal is to move into a manager role this year, and I'd appreciate your perspective and guidance."*

The best thing you can do to prepare is to practice. Not just once. Not just in your head. Say the words out loud, ideally to someone else, many, many times.

This may seem weird or awkward, but hear me out. It matters. Asking for a promotion is unlikely to be top of your conversation topics day in and day out. It isn't a conversation you'll have many times in your career. But it matters. Yes, it's going to feel awkward at first. Yes, you will be nervous. Yes, the stakes will feel high. Yes, asking for something is hard. Practicing will make a real difference.

So, here's how to do it. My first piece of advice is to record yourself. Put your phone or laptop camera to use and record yourself making the ask. Saying the words out loud cements them.

In addition, watching a recording yourself allows you to check out your body language and adjust if you need to.

If you can, after you've reviewed your recordings, ask someone you trust to role-play the conversation with you. This will allow you to get comfortable with making the ask and how to respond to questions.

Step 10: Ask for It

As a final step, schedule a meeting with your manager and let them know in advance that you'd like to discuss your performance.

I encourage you to make the ask for a promotion in a meeting versus in an e-mail. Having a dialogue is essential. Meeting in person, or over video, allows you to present your case most effectively. In addition, you will be able to assess the response when you can see the other person's body language as well as hear how they frame their words.

- Start with the promotion request first. The best approach is to only discuss salary when you know the role is yours.
- Use your prepared and practiced pitch. Remember to smile. Be mindful of your body language. Speak clearly and concisely.
- **And then stop talking!**
- Wait for the response. Stay calm, positive, and professional during the ask, regardless of what you hear in response.

Be prepared to be patient. Promotions take time and can involve multiple conversations. Depending on your organizational structure, your manager may need to make the case for your promotion to their boss as a next step. Don't be disheartened if your manager needs time to reflect, review, and discuss with others. Throughout the process, take time to listen and absorb all the feedback you receive from your manager. Your manager's perspective is pivotal in the moment, but you ultimately control your career, the opportunities you seek, and how you navigate toward your next big step.

Promotion conversations can feel petrifying because there's so much at stake. I get it, but I want you to continue to pursue what you want relentlessly. Focus on what you can control—your next steps—versus the array of possible outcomes. Following the 10-step promotion push strategy provides a framework for action. Your career growth plan will continue to evolve as it's the epicenter for your goals.

Lay the groundwork for a promotion by fine-tuning your communication skills and by making sure that you and your work are visible to decision makers. Review the role requirements for your next step and research salary brackets so that you have the information you need when the time comes. Align yourself with advocates who can help and do your own due diligence by understanding your employer's promotion process and cycles.

Prepare to ask for the role you want by assembling your accomplishments, creating your promotion proof points, and practicing the promotion conversation. Be prepared for pushback. Be prepared to negotiate.

It may not come easy. You may be supported. You may be doubted. You may be recognized. You may be disappointed. Keep pushing regardless. Hold on to what you're building toward, and don't be afraid to ask for what you want. Prep for it. Ask for it. Don't give up. Keep setting goals.

What's your next big step?

Q&A

Here are some questions I've received from people who were pursuing their own promotions.

I've been in my role for what feels like forever, but I've not been promoted yet. What do I do if my manager isn't supportive of advancing my career?

Try to analyze the reasons for the lack of support objectively. Take a step back and consider your responses to the following questions:

■ Has your manager referenced performance issues?
■ Are there things you need to do differently or better?
■ What's your manager's leadership style?
■ How would you assess your working relationship?
■ What external factors may impact promotion opportunities?

Sometimes considering the broader picture can help you identify ways to move forward. If your performance is perceived to be strong, but there's still a disconnect and your manager isn't supporting you, then you need to understand why. Set up a meeting to ask your manager for feedback on your professional development. This may be hard, but ask and then you'll have something to work with. It's in your best interest, while you are both in your respective roles, to get to the heart of why your manager is not supportive of you.

If you are not being supported, and think it's unfair, it's time to consider all your options and be strategic. You can only focus on what you can control. If your manager lacks the skills, ability, or desire to support you, it's time to evaluate your career options.

While your relationship with your manager is a key component to your success in your current role, you are ultimately responsible for your professional development. No one else will hold you accountable to your career goals. You need to prioritize what you want and commit to do what it will take to get you closer to what you want.

Your current manager will be in your orbit for a moment in time. Your career is yours to define. Build your networks inside and outside the company. Focus on your goals. Consider all your options. Do the work, and if you do the work well, it can only benefit you in the long term.

Please remember, you cannot allow a bad manager, or a poor relationship with your manager, to crush your spirit and stop you from doing your best work.

I just found out my coworker is being promoted, and I'm so upset. I want to know why I wasn't considered. Should I ask my boss?

It hurts when a role you've wanted so badly is given to someone else. Take time to process your emotions privately. Don't vent publicly, as you'll live to regret an emotional outburst. Instead, take time to consider your next steps.

Remember that it's not a race, and you can use this setback as a catalyst to move you forward. Talk to your manager about what success looks like for the role you are targeting. If you haven't done so already, share your career goals. Remember, your request for a promotion should not be based on what someone else has achieved, even though that might sting. Your promotion should be based on your attributes and results.

While I know it's hard not to, try to avoid comparing yourself directly to others. Focus on your strengths and the areas you want to develop. Turn your attention back to yourself, but not in a negative way. If the career you are coveting lands on someone else's plate, it doesn't mean you can't or won't achieve your goals too.

Make a career plan. Think about the skills you want to develop. Think about where you can add value. Think about problems you can solve for your team. Think about how you can become more visible. Think about how you show up at work and what you want to be known for. Demonstrate you're a good team player. Congratulate your coworker and stay laser focused on your goals. Channel your energy into your own next steps.

I found the courage to ask for a promotion, and I was told that I'm not ready. I'm devastated. What do I do next?

Being passed over for promotion hurts. Take the time you need to reflect, but don't give up. Ask for specific, actionable feedback that you can use to create a career growth plan. Focus on yourself and what you need to do next. You may decide to remain in your current role and work toward creating a future opportunity, you may decide to explore other opportunities, or you may decide to do both.

Decide on your goal and channel your energy into building your future. Raise the bar higher. Focus on your professional development goals, strive to do your best work, build a support network with advocates, and don't let the setback derail you.

Use the disappointment to motivate you to keep pushing forward. Don't shrink. Keep doing the work you need to do to invest in your career. Remember, if you don't continue to ask for new opportunities, your employer won't know that you are committed to advancing your career.

I've just been offered a promotion, but it wasn't something I'd asked for. What should I do?

First, congratulations! Take some space and time to consider how it feels. Are you elated? Daunted? A bit of both?

Review the role description and consider what excites you, or what doesn't excite you, about the opportunity. Then schedule a meeting to address any questions you have with your boss. If you will have a new boss because of the promotion, understand it may take time for you to forge a new relationship. Even though you know the company, it's still a new job. In this moment, take time to review and understand what the new role entails, what you need to do more of, continue to do, and what you need to let go of.

When you understand the role fully, ask for a meeting to review the compensation. In advance of that, do your own research to understand the industry salary ranges for your new role and be ready to negotiate the salary and associated benefits for your new position.

Establish how your promotion affects the team you work with currently, what you'll need to stop doing to fulfill your new responsibilities, and how your new role will be announced and introduced. As things progress, set yourself interim goals for your new role and continue to work on your career roadmap by setting new goals.

I just got promoted and the recognition feels like the biggest reward. Should I still negotiate my salary?

I always recommend negotiating, because if you have an offer, you have nothing to lose. Remember, your promotion won't be taken away from you. If you're happy with the initial compensation offer that accompanies your promotion, you should still do your homework—research the numbers. That way, you'll understand where your offer falls within the salary ranges for your industry.

On average, women continue to earn less than men. The gender pay gap disparity is even more pronounced for women of color. Because we are the most underrepresented group in the corporate pipeline, understanding our worth is more important than ever.

If your compensation offer falls short of the salary ranges uncovered from your research, share this with your boss and be ready to detail the sources so they know you've done your due diligence. In addition to negotiating a raise, there could be other benefits, bonuses, or stock options that could be part of your compensation package. If you don't ask, you won't get.

5

How to Navigate a Career Break

While I was writing this book, McKinsey & Company and LeanIn.org released a study stating one in four women were considering downshifting their careers or leaving the workforce completely due to COVID-19.[1] Prior to the start of the COVID-19 pandemic, figuring out whether and how to step back from your career was already hard. With the rapid ramifications of a public health emergency and a social and economic crisis, for many women stepping back from their workplaces became a necessity.

In chapter 2 we discussed how to bounce back from losing a job. Making a conscious decision to halt your career is just as challenging, with far-reaching consequences. Maybe you're planning to expand your family. Maybe you have a loved one you need to care for. Maybe you want to pursue further education. Or maybe you just straight up need a sabbatical. Leaving your professional comfort zone isn't easy, even if the ball is in your court. Taking a break in your career can be a tough call to make.

Usually, we start with the question, "Can I afford to give up my job right now?" Calculating the cost of time out, however, means accounting for more than simply the amount you receive in your biweekly or monthly paycheck. Did you know that if you stopped working for five years to have a family, it could cost you almost half a million dollars over the course of your career?

According to the Center for American Progress, the average American woman who takes a five-year career break to care for a child at age 26 will lose $467,000 over her working career.[2] The Center for American Progress created an interactive calculator that demonstrates just how much a career break will cost. By entering your age, salary, and the estimated length of your break, the online tool measures lost income growth, retirement assets, and benefits.[3] Designed by economist Michael Madowitz, the calculator shows the true cost of leaving the workforce temporarily.

So, what do you do if you need to take a career break, despite the math? The data on the cumulative impact of lost earnings, wage growth, and retirement benefits is startling, but often the driving factors for a career break outweigh the ramifications of reducing your income.

This chapter will help you plan for a career break and how to restart your career when you're ready to return.

Preparing for a Career Break

Every year, scores of women face one of the biggest hurdles in their personal and professional lives completely alone. But you are not alone. Knowledge is power. As women of color in the workplace, we are already earning less than we should be. It's crucial to be informed about what your career break could mean and the steps you can take to protect your long-term earning potential.

Review Policies and Legislation to Understand Your Options

Review your employer's HR policies so that you understand your requirements as an employee and what options might be available to you. If you'd like to return to your role, explore whether there are options for you to take paid or unpaid leave.

The Family and Medical Leave Act is a federal law that provides eligible employees of covered employers with unpaid, job-protected leave for specified family and medical reasons. For the first time at a federal level, the United States provided paid sick leave as part of the Families First Coronavirus Response Act in 2020.[4] The emergency measures were designed to support American workers who needed to take time off work due to COVID-19.

Employment law changes frequently. In addition to federal legislation, there is a patchwork of policies that are determined by employers, state, and local laws, or negotiated through labor contracts. As a result, it's vital to review your employer's policies and the legislation in your state to understand your rights.

Finalize Your Financial Plan

If you're preparing for an extended career break, you'll need to create a financial plan. Here are some important questions you should ask yourself as you consider your options.

The ideal scenario is to have enough savings to cover you for the duration of your break. If that scenario doesn't apply in this instance, it's time to create a plan that will sustain you. Identify if there are ways you could bring in income during your career break. Could you freelance or take on part-time work? If so, explore the options and try them out before you leave to see what's viable and how much you can make. Tiffany Aliche, founder of The Budgetnista and an award-winning teacher of financial education, recommends creating "a worst-case scenario contingency plan." She advises that setting up a game plan ahead of time will make you more confident if something bad does happen during your career break.[5]

If you don't have an emergency fund or a second income to help cover your expenses, your plan will need to be watertight. Determine how much money you spend each month. Track your spending behavior. Review your budget carefully, identify where you can cut back and the sacrifices you can make. If you have debt, aim to clear as much as you can before you take time off. Determine how you will cover your debt payments while you're not working and, wherever possible, avoid getting into any additional debt.

You will also need to consider your options for covering health insurance. If you have a partner, can you join their plan? You may also be eligible to join a parent's health insurance policy, dependent on your age. If not, you will need to review as many private insurance policy options as possible to find the one that best meets your needs.

In addition, you may need to consider your retirement contributions and savings. Reviewing your budget will help you determine if you plan to contribute to a retirement plan during your career break. I'm not a financial adviser—I'm a career coach—so I can't advise you on the best retirement options. If in doubt, talk to a financial adviser to review your situation. It's hard to assess a decision if you are not clear on the numbers or the best course of action.

It's vital that you go into a career break knowing how you will cover your bases. I want you to have your eyes wide open, so that you can fully embrace your decision and create a career plan that works for you. Finalizing a plan will help you focus on what drove you to take the break in the first place.

Lia's Story ━━━━━━━━━━━━━━━━━━━━━━━━━━━━━

Lia had built a successful career as a social media manager. She transferred to her employer's Chicago office after she landed a big promotion. Lia loved everything the city had to offer. Then suddenly, when she turned 36, her dad suffered a stroke. Lia maxed out the paid leave to be by his side at the hospital. It was hard. Lia has no siblings and her parents had divorced over a decade ago. Her dad needed her, and she needed to be there.

When her paid leave ended, Lia returned to work remotely, but it was hard. She couldn't meet her deadlines and care for her dad at the same time. After a couple of months, Lia realized she needed to resign from her role to oversee her dad's care. Lia had a small amount of savings that would cover the next six months. She gave notice at her firm, ended her lease in Chicago, said goodbye to friends, and packed her belongings into a U-Haul. Because she was moving into her dad's home, Lia planned to use her emergency fund to cover their expenses while she helped her dad with his rehabilitation and started the process of looking for freelance work.

That was two years ago, and while the future is unpredictable, Lia is assessing her career options and continues to look for full-time work in her hometown. In her social media manager role, Lia used to earn $86,000. Since starting her career break two years ago, she's lost $172,000 in wages plus $125,472 in wage growth over the course of her career. Lia has been unable to maintain retirement contributions while caring for her dad. Her previous employer had provided a 5 percent 401(k) contribution, which means Lia has lost $102,293 in retirement assets and benefits over the course of her lifetime.[6]

Being there for her dad was Lia's primary concern; however, keeping track of the numbers helps Lia understand the impact of her career break on her financial future.

Restarting Your Career After a Break

When you're looking to kick-start your career again, looking for opportunities may feel overwhelming. After making the decision to get back in the game, you might feel under pressure to make progress as fast as you can. One of the first things you should do, before you leap into LinkedIn, is to take time to consider what you really want in your next role.

That's right, I want you to get picky. Being picky is important, because whatever happens next, you will work hard. You'll work hard to get the role and you'll work even harder in it. If you're going to feel under pressure, I want it to be worth it, because you're working your way into a role that's great for you.

To get things going, I have an exercise I like to call "Must Have and Must Not."

Create Your "Must Have" and "Must Not" List

This is where you get to have fun and detail the type of opportunities you want to explore. The type of work you are drawn to, the locations you would like to work in, what your environment will look like, how much will be in your bank account at the end of the month.

I want you to think deeply about everything that matters to you when it comes to your work. No holds barred.

To help you do this, here are some questions I'd like you to consider:

1. How much money do you want to make?
2. What type of locations do you want to work in?

3. What environments motivate you?
4. What type of hours could you see yourself doing?
5. Which skills do you want to develop?
6. What size company do you want to work for?
7. What type of corporate culture are you drawn toward?
8. Is there anything that's nonnegotiable for you?

Next, I want you to prioritize your responses to questions 1–7.

It's okay if it's hard to choose between some of them. For example, if earning more than a certain threshold is just as important as keeping your commute to under 45 minutes, money and location can both be #1.

For the nonnegotiables you listed in question 8, if there's something that rises to the top as an absolute number 1 dealbreaker, make sure to note it. You get to decide if your nonnegotiables hang as a pack or if there's stuff there that stands out.

I want you to do this exercise at the outset because your choices matter. When you fall into the swirl of résumés, applications, interviews, and all the waiting in between, you may start to second-guess yourself. Job hunting is hard. The resistance you may face while searching for work isn't because your choices are wrong. The resistance is because prospective employers also have their list of must-haves and must-nots, and the trick is to find the right fit for both of you. That doesn't happen overnight.

I don't want you to lose sight of what matters. Get real about what you want because your career is important. You deserve to focus on your must-haves and then plot the route to move toward your goals.

Explaining the Gap

If you're worried about how to explain a gap on your résumé, or how to even put together your résumé, take a deep breath. While you may feel like you're a weaker candidate compared to others who stayed in the game, remember this:

Your core competencies and accomplishments haven't changed. Remember what makes you brilliant. Be proud of your entire career journey, pre–, during, and post–career break.

Very few people maintain a perfect career path with zero gaps. Most hiring managers know this. A career break doesn't have to be a dealbreaker. There will be some hiring managers who don't like it, but it's likely you wouldn't want to work for employers with that mindset.

"So, tell me about the gap on your résumé." When this prompt comes up in a job interview, you don't have to panic. There's also no need to overshare. In advance of your interview, practice how you will respond. You can write your response down, tweak it, and then practice it. Literally say it out loud, again and again and again, until you feel comfortable and can deliver the explanation with confidence. Record yourself saying it, so you can review your body language. I want you to be ready to provide a confident, concise overview outlining why you left your last role, what you've done since, and what you are looking to do next.

Explain the situation clearly but briefly. Keep it positive and action oriented, highlight your achievements, and you will be a compelling candidate.

Here's a template you can follow during your response to the career break question:

- Highlight a key achievement from your last role.
- Explain briefly why you left.
- Explain briefly what you've done since.
- Share any relevant skills you acquired during your career break.
- Emphasize why you are returning to work now, explaining why you're excited to return to your industry.
- Reaffirm your most relevant skills and bring the focus back to what you can deliver for this employer.

You don't need to apologize for your career break or justify it. Instead, focus on what you bring to the table and the impact your skills will have on their organization. If you focus on comparing yourself with other candidates, your career break will feel like an obstacle. That's a perception and not a fact. If your career break was shorter than the sum of your professional experience, there's no reason for you to feel it should be a bigger deal than it is. You wouldn't be called to interview in the first place if you weren't a strong candidate. Recruiters don't have time to waste.

You can also use your cover letter to explain your career gap if you choose to. If you do that, be clear and direct. Just one sentence should cover it. Not all cover letters are read, so it's smart to be ready to explain a gap, if asked.

The most important thing is to be honest. Don't try and hide a career gap by overextending your start or end dates on your résumé. A lie on your résumé will come back to haunt you as your prospective employer will verify your employment history before extending an offer.

Create a Compelling Career Statement

A career statement at the top of your résumé can reinforce what makes you a strong candidate and set the tone for the supporting proof points in your résumé. It's not mandatory to use one, but it can be a highly effective addition to your cover letter and your résumé. As mentioned earlier, you can also use it to explain your career break.

An introductory career statement serves as a concise and compelling introduction. More importantly, it reinforces why someone should hire you. A career statement highlights your most relevant expertise in a few sentences, detailing your exceptional qualities, skills, experience, and how you've added value or produced results. Your statements should be tailored toward the job you are targeting and encapsulate why you are the perfect candidate for the role.

If you're not sure that you need one, you can always decide on a case-by-case basis. Trust your instincts. If you believe you can sell yourself more effectively with a career statement, then use one.

If you decide to add one, here's how to do it:

1. Take an inventory of your accomplishments in your most relevant roles and examine the skills you used to generate your results.
2. Analyze the requirements of the job you are targeting and look for examples where your skills and expertise overlap.
3. Select adjectives that describe your key strengths, and make sure to avoid repetition.
4. Weave the key strength adjectives into your desired role requirements, with your accomplishments as proof points.

For example, this is how a product marketing professional created her career statement:

Key accomplishments
- Earning the trust of difficult and demanding clients led to management of six-figure budgets
- Leading complex product launches and delivering results with remote teams

Key strengths
- Communication skills
- Can-do attitude, great at motivating others
- International experience

Requirements of the target role
- Global account management
- Financial forecasting
- Team building

Final statement:

A senior marketing leader with demonstrated success in delivering FMCG product launches in over 15 markets with an annual budget of $750K+. Adept at building and motivating teams, leveraging respected communication and management skills.

And that's it. If you follow these steps you will have a career statement that is targeted to the role you are applying for.

Naomi's Story

It wasn't an easy decision to quit her six-figure job in data analytics, but after a decade of long hours, constant deadlines, and a less than stellar corporate culture, Naomi needed a reset. She resigned from her role and used her time away to reconnect with her passion for cooking and to think about what to do next.

Naomi knew her break needed an expiration date, and then she would need to find work fast. However, she didn't want to make the same mistake and end up in an environment that was the wrong fit. During her time away, Naomi realized she was interested in exploring data analyst roles at creative companies. When Naomi was in the final two months of her break, she switched gears and got right down to business. She used her downtime to reach out to friends in her network for insights to help determine what she would do next.

Next, Naomi spent a weekend scrolling through her Instagram and Twitter to remove any posts that were borderline unprofessional. She brainstormed new content she could share on LinkedIn with her take on data analytics trends and industry developments. She updated her social media bios to make them consistent and added the link to her new website. Naomi knew hiring managers would do an online search. She wanted to make sure the search engine optimization results reflected her skills and expertise versus her culinary adventures.

Leverage Your Network

Networking may feel like a scary prospect, especially when you've been out of work for an extended time. I get that, but set up some video calls and check out some events anyway.

One way to approach networking is to think of it as "valuable conversations with positive and helpful people." Networking is less daunting if you break it down to what it really is—keeping in touch and sharing resources, ideas, and information.

Even if you don't intend to return to a previous employer, it's still advantageous to connect with former managers and coworkers. First, you will need references, so it's smart to let your former manager hear from you before they are cold contacted by a recruiter. Second, your former coworkers are likely to have tons of connections and suggestions that could help you with your search.

People in your circle can provide valuable support, but they can only do that if they know what you are looking for. And even if someone is unable to help in the moment, simply knowing the direction you are moving in will plant a seed. If your contacts don't know what you are looking for, they won't be able to keep you top of mind for opportunities they may see that could be great for you.

Don't be afraid to reach out to start conversations, even if you feel like you're in a position of weakness. It's likely you'll be surprised by the outcome, and you can also help others, which will give you a feel-good, paying-it-forward kind of boost and cement your value.

Use Social Media in a Smart Way

Social media platforms are indispensable tools for keeping up to speed on what's happening in your industry and forging connections. You can see what your network is working on or excited about, and those insights can be incredibly valuable.

On the flip side though, as we know, social media can have several negative effects. It's relatively easy to fall into the trap of comparing your career progress to the other people. We all get struck with career envy at some point, and usually when we least expect it. You log on to LinkedIn to research a job opportunity and the first thing on your feed is a humblebrag announcement from a former coworker celebrating their dazzling ascent up the corporate ladder. It happens, and if it stings a little don't let that throw you off course. Keep focused on your next steps and before you know it, you'll have a new announcement to share on LinkedIn too.

In the interim, while you're moving through the job search process, it's essential to be mindful of how you present yourself on social media platforms. Don't mix professional contacts or conversations with personal ones, and don't share or post anything that could come back to haunt you in the future.

When you're happy with your résumé, make sure your LinkedIn profile aligns with what you've shared. It's also smart to do an audit of your social media profiles to scrub them of anything that shouldn't really be there or turn them private if you need to. If you use a portfolio or personal website to showcase your work, now is a great time to update those too.

Identify Recruiters You Can Target

In recent years recruiting companies, such as Après, reacHIRE, and iRelaunch, have launched with the specific mission of connecting employers with returning career breakers. In addition, companies are starting to realize they can do more to help women who are looking to reignite their careers. As a result, a vast array of employers, ranging from Johnson & Johnson to Mastercard, are offering return-to-work programs.

It's also smart to identify recruiters who specialize in your industry sector. Your network, coupled with professional industry associations and publications, will be a great resource to help you figure out which recruiters should be on your radar.

Jessica's Story ━━━━━━━━━━━━━━━━━━━━━━━

After leaving her career in video production to care for her baby, Jessica planned to return to work as soon as her daughter was in preschool. But her plans changed overnight when her husband was furloughed and suddenly Jessica needed to find work fast.

In a panic, Jessica reached out to her former company hoping to return, but since her departure the production company had lost key clients and her manager had been laid off. At home, bills were piling up and Jessica was so anxious that she couldn't sleep. She spent hours and hours on job boards but struggled to find openings she could apply for. When she did see a job posting, her confidence plummeted at the thought of competing against candidates who didn't have gaps on their résumés. Jessica didn't know how to explain why she stepped away from her career or how to convince anyone that she was worth hiring.

At the beginning, Jessica was determined to spend all day, every day on her laptop looking for jobs. She signed up for job posting e-mail alerts and spent hours in front of her screen checking and refreshing bookmarked job boards. After the first week Jessica was exhausted, and her job search felt like it was going nowhere. Five months later, Jessica started to wonder if she needed to rethink her entire career.

By chance, while running errands with her daughter, Jessica ran into a former client from her old firm. At first her heart sank, as she didn't want to talk about résumés, applications, or anything career related. But Jessica's former client sensed how stressed she was. She gently suggested that Jessica attend an event she was working on for women in creative industries. She promised it would be informal and low key. Jessica took her advice. Halfway through the event, Jessica connected with a production assistant who in turn referred Jessica to a recruiter. That referral led to a phone interview—Jessica's first tangible lead in months.

Create a Job Search Schedule

Even when you're feeling motivated, job hunting can be daunting. Creating a routine will help you set some boundaries and be productive. Block out time for certain tasks and set small, measurable goals for yourself. Keep a record of what you accomplish each day so you can track your progress.

It can be easy to underestimate the time it takes to search for open opportunities, complete application forms, or prep for interviews. Keep track of what you do to help you stay motivated. Give yourself breaks by intersperperingjob hunting with activities you enjoy. Remember you can't be "on" all the time. Take time to listen to podcasts, read books, and use webinars that can help you prep for interviewing.

When you're planning your job search schedule, think of activity-driven tasks that allow you to take a break from scrolling endlessly through job postings for hours. You could start to edit your wardrobe to put together interview outfits or set up a video chat with a friend to complete a mock interview.

If you feel like your job hunt is going nowhere fast, focus on what you *can* control, as opposed to what you can't. Maintaining a positive mindset is the secret to working through the search. Your mindset is the most important variable in the recruitment process. It's also the only variable you have full control over. You can't control other people's actions, but you can control how you respond to them.

If you're not getting interviews here are three things you can do:

1. **Keep polishing your résumé, cover letter, and application materials.**

   Ask people you trust in roles you are targeting for feedback on edits you can make to your materials.

2. **Be targeted.**

   Focus on the opportunities for which you are an ideal fit, where your skill set and experience align squarely.

3. **Be confident.**

   Don't give up, even if you're feeling disheartened. Do an activity you enjoy and then get back on track.

If you're getting interviews, but they're not leading to offers, here's the advice I give to my coaching clients:

1. **You're on the right track.**

   Interview practice is always valuable. Remember, you wouldn't be called to interview in the first place if you couldn't do the role.

2. **Learn from each experience.**

   If you were nervous or couldn't answer a key question, learn from the experience, and you will be better equipped for your next interview. Assess what you can take from the situation and apply those insights to your next job opportunity.

3. **Don't give up.**

   Keep looking for opportunities where you can show your next employer what you bring to the table.

The recruitment cycle can be rough. Unfortunately, there's no way around that. It's often a marathon versus a sprint, and you need to be prepared for what could be a long haul before you get to where you want to be. If you want the role that's right for you, you should be prepared to invest the time, resources, and effort it will take to land it. Maintaining a positive mindset will be the best thing you can do as you work through it.

Negotiating Your Salary After a Career Break

Receiving an offer for a new role is a moment to savior. In the excitement of securing an opportunity, I want to make sure you land the salary you deserve, as discussed in chapter 3.

Not only are women more likely to take parental, family, or medical leave than men, they are more likely to experience a negative impact on their career as a result. Women are nearly twice as likely to say taking time off had a negative impact on their job or career as compared with men.[7] During the COVID-19 crisis, childcare and home-schooling responsibilities were disproportionately shouldered by women. *The Impact of COVID-19 on Women*, a policy brief issued by the United Nations, concluded that women will be the hardest hit by this pandemic, but they will also be the backbone of recovery in communities.[8]

The contingent factors that affect how we build our careers and balance our commitments raise the stakes even higher. Ensuring we do whatever it takes to negotiate our salaries matters more than ever before.

In chapter 3, I shared how to land on your Target Salary Range, how to create your Pay Me More Proof Points, and scripts you can use to make your ask. Revisit the recommendations so that you are ready to negotiate when an offer comes through. And remember, if you don't ask, you don't get.

Navigating a career break is hard, but hard is not impossible. Career paths don't necessarily follow a linear trajectory. There can be acceleration, pauses, and phases that may feel like you're moving backwards. Careers will ebb and flow, and where you are in a moment in time is not where you will be forever. If you are embarking on a career break, or returning to work following a career break, fully embrace your decision and make a career plan that works for you. No one else will know how your career feels. The experience is unique to you.

Taking a career break will have an impact on your finances, but with careful planning before you depart, strategic planning during your job search, and solid networking and negotiation skills, you can and will land your next role and continue to push forward.

Q&A

Here are some questions I've been asked about navigating a career break.

I'd love to return to work, but I need flexible schedule options because I'm still caring for my father. I don't know where to start. What should I do?

As a first step, keep your needs front and center, because that's the most important part. Get clear on what you need from your next role; that list may include preferences related to the location, hours, type of work, responsibilities, salary, culture, and benefits.

The "Must Have" and "Must Not" exercise within this chapter will help you determine what matters most, in addition to the work schedule. It will also help you identify components you may be able to sacrifice to get what matters most in your next role.

When you're clear on what you need, focus your job search on opportunities that align with your priorities.

As you work through next steps, talk to others who are in similar positions and ask for advice and recommendations. A suggestion or recommendation may spark a new approach or previously unknown opportunity.

I'm about to start applying for roles, and so many people are also looking for work. How can I compete with candidates who don't have gaps on their résumés?

Dealing with pressure due to demand for roles is tough, but don't create your own ceiling. I encourage you to be proud of all your experiences, during your career and during your break. Just because you have a gap on your résumé doesn't mean you're a second-tier candidate.

Practice explaining the gap on your résumé and create a compelling career statement that allows your skills and achievements to shine. Remember, being in between jobs happens to almost everyone at some stage in their career. You still have a valuable contribution to make. Don't worry about what comes next, just take it one step at a time. Keep looking for opportunities where you can show your next employer what you can bring to the table.

Through my work as a career coach, I spend a significant amount of time helping candidates polish their interview responses, harness positive body language, and tap into their key attributes that will set them up for success in the interview cycle. If your confidence has taken a hit, tap into as many resources as you can to help with your career goals. If one-to-one career coaching isn't an option, identify a friend to be a sounding board during your job search or a former coworker with whom you can discuss what's happening in your industry. You don't have to go it alone, and connecting with others will help you when you need a boost.

I'm worried that I've fallen behind during my break. How can I rebuild my confidence?

To help boost your self-confidence, review your list of career accomplishments. Achievements don't expire, because the attributes and skills you used to do great things are inherently in you. Doing everything you can to maintain a positive mindset is paramount, because it's the one variable over which you have full control. Instead of second-guessing your present, focus on your future. Create an action plan for your next set of career goals.

Learning a new skill is a fast way to boost your confidence and your résumé. Brainstorm topics that interest you and will enhance your career. There are scores of online resources at your fingertips. For example, Udemy provides a global marketplace of tens of thousands of online video courses, with new additions published every month. Also, Coursera has partnered with top universities from around the world, including Yale University, Johns Hopkins University, and the University of Edinburgh, to provide hundreds of online courses, from computer science to financial accounting and beyond.

Making the decision to learn something new will demonstrate to prospective employers that you're a self-starter, so it's a win-win all round.

6

Achieving Your Goals While Caring for Your Family

Work is stressful at the best of times. Dealing with your career while being a caregiver or working parent can feel like a constant tug-of-war. Too many of us feel like the rope is about to fray and we're bracing ourselves for the breaking point.

I wrote this book while my daughters' school was closed for almost a year during the coronavirus pandemic. Families everywhere were left reeling by a global health emergency coupled with an unprecedented child-care crisis while trying to hang on to their jobs. The pandemic laid bare the depth of the inequities for caregivers and working parents. It's been the hardest of times.

Working parenthood was already hard before the pandemic. Adjusting to caregiving can be sudden and debilitating. It's an extremely personal and often challenging experience to navigate while trying to maintain a career. It's no surprise that our stress levels can fly off the charts.

According to the National Partnership for Women and Families, the racial wealth gap means that families of color have, on average, fewer resources than white families to plan for and absorb the effects of a serious personal or family medical issue, including the birth or adoption of a new child.[1] Our communities tend to experience greater health needs, coupled with more caregiving responsibilities.

Yes, it's a universal issue. But it doesn't make it right. The unfairness of the systemic challenges makes me angry. The hard truth is, as a baseline, working parents and caregivers do not have the support they deserve. Here in the United States, parental leave legislation lags almost every industrialized country in the world. Navigating the care system can be a nightmare, while eroding caregivers' financial well-being and health, and affecting their work. According to the American Association of Retired Persons (AARP), one out of every five American adults provide care to someone else in a given year.[2] On top of this, statistics show women of color are more likely to be key and sole breadwinners for their families, often at the same time they are primary caregivers for their loved ones. This means, for many of us, taking a career break or quitting a job isn't an option.

So how do you balance your career as a parent, a caregiver, or both?

Iris's Story

Iris loved her job. She'd worked hard for it. She was the first person in her family to go to college, and she'd known all along that when the time came, she would start a family and keep her career. Iris met her partner a few years ago through her work. They were both driven and focused on building a future for their family. Their respective paths hadn't been easy. Iris was one of very few women in her division and no one else shared her background. By now, she was used to that and felt she'd earned the respect of her peers based on her ability to move quickly and close leads. Her manager told her she was an asset, and she consistently exceeded her quotas each quarter.

Now, Iris felt she was going to lose everything she'd worked so hard for. Everyone in her family was so elated when she announced she was having a baby. Her pregnancy had been relatively smooth, and Iris's company offered paid leave, which she gratefully took. She kept in touch with her team intermittently during her time away while finding her feet as a new mom. Iris's cousins recommended a few child-care providers, and she was able to secure a spot for her son with her first choice.

It had been a whirlwind year, but everything had gone right. Until Iris returned to work. She had been away for almost three months, and in her final two weeks of leave, she started to mentally prepare for jumping right back in. And here she was, sitting in a cubicle in the restroom trying not to cry.

Iris had kept in touch with her manager during her leave, but he hadn't informed her that three of her biggest accounts that she'd delegated to a coworker during her absence would remain that way. Iris was devastated. Her manager wanted her to focus on two new projects instead, but they weren't part of her territory and it felt like a step back. She knew she'd been gone, but she was counting on picking up where she left off. It wasn't just her ego that was hurt; losing the accounts meant losing her commissions. On top of it all, Iris was exhausted. She spent her nights trying to untangle the new project while pumping bottles for her baby. She had no idea how to do either with ease. Iris was so frustrated she just wanted to scream. When her tears did fall, Iris felt betrayed. She'd worked so hard for so long and followed all the rules during her pregnancy, and yet here she was, feeling like a failure.

A week later, a former college friend who worked close by asked Iris if they could meet for coffee. Iris appreciated the suggestion and confided how hard things had been. Her friend had taken parental leave a year earlier. She consoled Iris and told her nursing a baby and working is tough, but that it won't last forever. She also assured Iris that her career wasn't over. She asked if Iris had created a return-to-work plan with her supervisor. Iris paused, realizing they had created a handover plan with lots of care, but that was it. When it came to transitioning back to work, they'd only agreed on a return-to-work date.

Iris realized it wasn't too late to have a conversation. She decided she would ask for a meeting with her supervisor to create a transition plan and share some of the opportunities she'd love to pursue again. In the interim, she listened closely to her friend's advice and realized she needed to give herself more space and time to adjust to being back at work as a new mom. She immediately felt a bit better and asked her friend if they could start meeting for lunch on a weekly basis.

If you're feeling overwhelmed or conflicted about how you will move forward at work, I'd like to share a four-step approach to help you create a career plan that best supports you.

Step 1: Set New Career Commitments

Step 2: Set Yourself Up for Success

Step 3: Create Your Personal Career Care Plan

Step 4: Assess, Acknowledge, and Adjust

Each step is designed to help you navigate a short-term or longer-term life shift while continuing to invest in and cultivate your career.

Step 1: Set New Career Commitments

Your parental or caregiving responsibilities will require you to adjust how you approach your work. Often, we are focused on what our employer needs, what our role requires, and how to hold everything together while navigating our additional family or parental demands. Your circumstances have shifted, sometimes in ways that are rapidly evolving, and those changes will have an impact.

It's a lot to get your head around, but what I'd love for you to also do is to take a step back and consider your career from your new perspective. This might feel a bit overwhelming at first, so I want to help you create a set of commitments centered squarely on you, to help anchor you.

Here are a set of 12 questions that I'd like you to take a moment to ask yourself. Take note of your responses and hold space to reflect on what you identify.

1. What do you want to accomplish at work in the next three, six, or nine months?
2. What are your immediate priorities?
3. What are your immediate concerns?
4. What would success look like for you?
5. What's your preferred work schedule?
6. What would help you to do your best work?
7. What are some obstacles/challenges you need to address?
8. What is within your control?

9. Where do you need help or support for your caregiving or parental responsibilities?
10. What are your boundaries and how will you protect them?
11. What will you commit to do next?
12. What do you need to ask for?

Then, after you've reflected on your responses, I'd like you to complete the following four sentences and write down your responses in a safe place where you can go back to review them when needed. In chapter 9 you'll find a blank Career Commitments worksheet you can use.

By completing this, you will create a set of personal pledges that are uniquely yours to anchor how you will move forward. These will be your career commitments that are specific to your current needs and circumstances.

Your Career Commitments

I am doing this work because . . .
    To do my best work and feel like I'm thriving,
I need to . . .
    When I hit an obstacle, I will remember . . .
    The work I'm doing is laying the foundation for
me to . . .

I encourage you to review these regularly and go back to redo the exercise as often as needed. Parental and caregiving responsibilities can shift rapidly, and so can career demands. You may need to continue to update and revise your intentions and commitments as you progress.

You can still create goals for your career, and they should reflect your needs as a caregiver. Goals don't need to be set in stone forever. Deal with the here and now and reassess and realign goals and commitments at future intervals.

Step 2: Set Yourself Up for Success

The next step is to set yourself up for success. How you do this will of course be affected by the requirements of your role and your environment, but I want you to identify the areas you can control and what you need to set yourself up to do your best work.

Review your responses to questions 4 through 12 in Step 1.

What did you identify as some of the obstacles you're currently facing? What help or support do you need right now? What did you identify as being within your control?

In addition to detailing your work hours, what boundaries will you need to put in place? How will you honor those?

Reflect on your response to:

"To do my best work and feel like I'm thriving, I need to . . ."

What's the next step you can take to support this?

Be Prepared to Ask for What You Need

If you need to make an ask from your employer, you should create an opportunity to start a dialogue with your boss.

For example, you may realize that you need to make your supervisor aware of your caregiving situation. You might have come to the realization that you need to adjust your hours. Perhaps you want to transition from a full-time to part-time position, or maybe you need a temporary flexible schedule. If you've identified something that lies out of your own direct control to take action, don't be afraid to ask. I know this can be a scary prospect, but you need to remember your situation or circumstance has shifted considerably, creating changes you are responding to and endeavoring to problem-solve as effectively as possible.

In addition to preparing your ask, you need to prepare to be your own best advocate. A conversation will provide a space for you to understand your supervisor's expectations and is an opportunity to get their guidance, as and when needed, on the parameters for you to do your best work.

If you need to approach your manager with an ask related to adjusting your schedule, here are some tips to help you summon the courage and prepare for the conversation:

- Review your employee handbook to understand policies and protocols, so you know the parameters for your organization.
- Assess your performance to date and make sure there aren't any outstanding issues or deliverables.
- Clarify what you want and think through in advance where you might be open to negotiation.
- Frame what you need from the company's perspective and try to find a win/win for your manager and for you. Emphasize the benefits to your organization by detailing what you will accomplish.
- Demonstrate your commitment to your role and provide evidence of your recent results.
- Put yourself in their shoes, think through the type of questions your manager may ask you, and prepare how you would respond.
- Consider ways you can forge trust and convey outcomes to prove things are working out, if the answer is "yes."
- Be ready to suggest a trial period to assess how it's working for you and your boss.
- Where possible, make this a direct conversation so you can have a dialogue, but don't expect to receive an immediate answer.

- Think through in advance how you'll respond to three possible outcomes:

  1. You get what you want.
  2. You are told "no."
  3. You are offered an alternative.

Ask for feedback and be ready listen closely to the suggestions or response.

Manage Your Expectations

I want you to remember there isn't a one-size-fits-all approach to how to do your best work. You may need to try a variety of approaches before you find the one that's right for you. Test things out and you can adjust if something doesn't work out.

A proof point is the time that's set on your alarm clock right now. And, if you don't have an alarm set . . . wow, I am so envious of you. But for a moment, think about the time you wake up to start your workday. Is it the exact same time as your boss, or a coworker? Maybe, maybe not, you may have no way of ever knowing. Even if it is the exact same time, how you wake up and what happens next is unique to you.

As a career coach, I'm often asked, "How can I be more productive?" or, "How can I accomplish more in my day?" Even though I'm a coach, I often ask myself these exact same questions. The truth is, I can't give you one technique that will make you more productive or help you knock out a to-do list faster. I wish I could, but I can't.

There are scores of productivity experts who share really smart suggestions on how to schedule time, tasks, track to-dos, and all of those things. I've tried a bunch of approaches and benefited from the experiments. From doing the worst first, to time-blocking tasks, to working for a set amount of time then taking a break. What's best for you will vary entirely on what your work entails, and you should explore what might help you based on where you're at and what you need.

But here, in this chapter, I don't want to tell you how to squeeze more hours out of your workday. I want to help you figure out what matters most and how to keep your career priorities at the forefront while doing what's needed for your employer and your caregiving or parental responsibilities.

I truly believe a pivotal part of achieving this is managing expectations, starting with your own.

The reason I can't give you the golden ticket to time management nirvana is because I'm terrible at it. I have a bad habit of creating daily to-do lists that assume I have five or six clones. A half dozen Octavias simultaneously churning away on a bunch of really pressing things. There's no way I can realistically do the things I often write down as my daily to-dos. And that perpetually sets me up for failure. Trying to do it all can feel like mission impossible.

Every so often balls get dropped, sometimes spectacularly, and I realize that I must reset my own expectations. Sometimes you need to know when to say no. Even to yourself.

Prioritization, of course, is essential. Cut out anything that isn't essential, but please remember that doesn't include cutting out sleep. Set boundaries and remember those boundaries are there to protect you. Get as much help as you can wrangle and figure out where you can delegate or drop tasks.

Step 3: Create Your Personal Care Plan

I'm obsessed with Pinterest, and a few years ago I created a private Pinterest board called the T.A.C.O. It wasn't about tacos, although I love those too. My board was about Taking Absolute Care of Octavia. I came to realize I needed visual reminders of the things

I needed to do to take care of myself while I was busy doing all the things I needed to do. For me, visuals are much more evocative than a list. I can see what I need, and that's powerful.

Honor What Fuels You

If you like visuals too, you can create your own motivational board, or if you prefer lists, do that instead. Whatever it takes, I want you to create your personal care plan and give it a name that's uniquely yours. It should include the support you need, resources you can leverage, strategies to replenish your energy, and the approach and mindset you need to thrive. The hardest part of being a caregiver, a working parent, or both simultaneously, is that your time outside of work is centered on taking care of others. Your needs can and will get put on the backburner, so it's vital you hold space for moments to think through how you can take care of yourself too.

Foster Relationships to Support You

The next thing I'd like you to do is cultivate relationships that can lift you up at work. Being a woman of color in the workplace is hard. Sometimes support and connections are few and far between. Pay attention to people around you who are role models and lead by example. Pay attention to people you've worked well with. Pay attention to people who have traits you admire.

I say this because when I was a full-time employee with an infant and a toddler to dash home to, I neglected to do this. I raced into work each morning, raced through my workday before racing home. I had a horribly long commute and every evening I needed to pick up both of my daughters from their respective child-care providers. I figured networking and connecting was something I just couldn't do. I didn't have the time. I was wrong. I was so isolated, so tired, and so miserable. Looking back, I now know wholeheartedly that what I needed was to spend some time in the orbit of others who could help me, even if they didn't realize it, just by observing how they navigated their way through our workplace. If I'd paid more attention, I'd have realized there were employee resource groups that met at lunchtime that I could have joined. It wasn't just about after-work drinks; there were other ways I could have forged connections that would have made my working-parent experience much less lonely.

Be intentional, though, about whom you lean on for advice. Finding a mentor is hard and finding the right mentor can sometimes be even trickier. Sadly, not all women are treated equally and without bias, even by other women. I recall meeting a new mentor for the very first time shortly after my first daughter was born. During our conversation I mentioned in passing that I had a baby. She immediately recoiled and told me it wouldn't be possible to do what I wanted to do with a baby. Instead of challenging her response, I was stunned into silence, my confidence crushed. I waited for an apology that never came; instead she picked up her phone and started checking her e-mail, signaling our conversation was over. I'd believed I was about to forge a relationship with someone who wanted to help me advance. Instead I was being judged and discriminated against by another woman.

Consider your relationships at work and invest time in the ones that are critical to your performance or inspire you. When your time is limited, it's important to be intentional with how you use it. You may not be able to join every after-hours event or gathering, but try to find ways to carve out occasional time and space for making connections that can support you.

Kendra's Story

Kendra didn't know what to do. A few months ago, her son had fractured his ankle after falling off his bike. She'd used her remaining vacation days to cover her time away from work while she took care of him. Now, her mom needed her help, and it was serious. What the family hoped would be a routine checkup turned into a follow-up, and then consulting a specialist, then more tests followed by a long wait before a diagnosis that no one had been prepared for.

Kendra was reeling. Her mom was the one who would step in to help whenever anyone needed it. She lived alone and had been fiercely independent, but now everything had changed almost overnight. Now, Kendra and her brother took turns stopping by their mom's home before work to check on her and alternated heading over after work to make sure she'd eaten.

After a few weeks it became apparent that her mom needed support during the day. Kendra had exhausted her PTO and didn't know how she could do it. She needed to be on-site for her job. It wasn't possible to be in two places at once. Kendra didn't want her supervisor to know what was going on. It had been hard enough when she had to take time away for her son, and now this. There had been rounds of layoffs and Kendra couldn't afford to lose her paycheck; her family needed it more than ever before to cover the medical bills her mom was facing.

That night, Kendra called her brother and told him they needed to round up the family and come together to discuss a caregiving plan for their mom. The next morning, Kendra summoned the courage to ask her supervisor if they could connect. She took a deep breath and told him that her mom was seriously ill and asked if there might be the opportunity to adjust her start and end times as she worked to figure out a care plan with her family, based around her mom's hospital appointments. Kendra was surprised to learn her supervisor had faced a similar situation before she joined the team. He told her he was confident they could find a way to make it work.

Think Through Crisis Contingency Support

I've been there. You're deep into an important task at work when your phone flashes. It's an emergency, someone needs you, and you need to leave to take care of it. There's also a flip side to that, where a meeting runs later than planned and just like that, there's no way you're going to get to day care before the final pickup time.

It's a horrible, horrible feeling. You are stuck between a rock and a hard place. When my daughters were small, I used to have a job that required me to travel around the country. I would plan the trips carefully to ensure my flight times aligned with our child-care arrangements. However, simultaneously my husband had a job that required him to travel internationally for work, often with less than 24 hours' notice.

On one of those occasions, my husband was on a last-minute trip to Korea while I was in Denver, supposedly headed home to Los Angeles where our babysitter was waiting. She had picked up our daughters from day care and preschool, given the girls dinner, put them to bed, and was waiting for me to get home. And then, of course, at the gate, I discovered my flight was delayed, and then delayed again. I was distraught. Luckily, the flight wasn't cancelled. I finally made it home hours late, and after giving our sitter a big tip, I collapsed in tears. The last few hours had been beyond stressful. I didn't have another backup if my babysitter couldn't have stayed longer. I realized in that moment I needed to rethink my contingency plans.

My recommendation is: on a good day, grab your favorite snack and sit down to make note of all the possible crisis scenarios you may have to deal with as a working parent or caregiver. Then, start to troubleshoot what options you may have to deal with each potential crisis. You'll quickly see where there are gaps you need to fill, and that will prompt where you can take preemptive actions.

One of the benefits of doing this is there's a psychological boost of having thought through what you would do "if." It's a bit like having the extra diaper bag in the car or knowing there's a fire extinguisher in the cupboard next to the stove. It will provide you with some peace of mind.

You should also check with your employer, as there may be caregiving resources, benefits, mental health support, or reimbursements you may not be aware of. Some employers offer on-site child care, some offer lists of backup child-care services, and some have relationships with caregiving providers that can offer discounts.

Step 4: Assess, Acknowledge, and Adjust

As I mentioned earlier in the chapter, your demands as a parent and caregiver can change rapidly. As a result, it's important to set regular intervals to review how things are working out for you. Don't wait for your performance review or a meeting with your manager to roll around before you do this. This is your career, and no one will be as invested in your success as you. When you have other demands it's hard to make time to review how you are doing. That's why even just a mini evaluation will pay dividends, so you don't lose completely sight of yourself during a turbulent or demanding time.

I recommend doing a check-in every month and paying extra attention at three-month intervals too. Revisit your career commitments and then write down your responses to these self-evaluation questions:

1. Do I need to make any changes to my career commitments? If so, what needs to adjust?
2. What has happened since my last check-in that I'm proud of?
3. What's working well for me right now?

4. What isn't working for me right now?
5. What's one thing I could do, or set in motion, to move me closer to a professional goal?
6. Who would I like to connect with in the next month?
7. On a scale of 1–5, with 5 being the best, how am I doing at maintaining my personal career care plan?

Acknowledgment is an essential part of building your career. You might think I'm referring to recognition from your manager, but I'm not. Getting kudos from a supervisor is always great, but I'm talking about self-acknowledgment.

There's so much of your career that's unseen. No one knows what it takes to get to work on time every day. No one knows what it takes to prepare for the start of a work week. No one knows what keeps you up at night when you finally get to bed.

I want you to create a list of rewards that you will promise to allocate to yourself when you've done something that matters. They can be small, they can big, they can be an experience that doesn't cost a thing, or a treat that requires a splurge. You get to decide. One strategy I've used for myself is writing out a list of things I'd love to do or treat myself to. Then I jotted each thing down on a small piece of paper, folded them up, and dropped them in a jar. When something cool happened, I'd reach into the jar, pull out a piece of paper, unfold it, read it, and do whatever it said to acknowledge my achievement. If I couldn't do it right away, I'd keep the piece of paper on my desk to remind me it was an action item that needed taking care of.

Stay true to what you want from your career and keep setting goals. In moments of stress and upheaval, you may not feel like this is possible. I understand. But there will come a time when you look back in awe at what you did while working as a parent or a caregiver. And, even if you feel like you're not achieving the things you had wanted to, sometimes a reset or pause can prove to be a catalyst. You just don't realize it in the moment.

You haven't lost your abilities, or drive, or talents. Your circumstances have shifted. Focus on your short-term priorities and be intentional about your professional and personal needs. When I was trying to figure out how to be a working mom for the first time, I didn't realize what I know now, with the benefit of a decade of hindsight. Becoming a parent made me a better worker. At the time I was so focused on my schedule, and how to squeeze in everything, that I failed to realize I was increasingly more efficient. I worked faster, mostly because I had to. I had to get everything that mattered done so I could jump in the car and fight traffic to execute two child-care pickups by 6 p.m. I was much more thorough, and I was more astute. The extra caregiving responsibilities I was handling weren't a limitation—they were an asset. But I only started to realize that many years later.

Let's stop and think about it for a moment, though. What do a ton of job descriptions often look for?

- Self-starter
- Problem-solver
- Team player
- Uses initiative
- Multitasker

The list goes on.

Chances are, as a caregiver or working parent, you're doing all these things before your day job even begins. Juggling isn't easy, but take pride in what you do and know that a few balls will drop sometimes.

On reflection, I know that the reason I struggled so much in the early years of being a working parent had a lot to do with fear of how I'd be perceived, coupled with crippling guilt. Maintaining a career with constraints can open a gateway to guilt that's tough to swallow. I felt mom guilt for working full-time and spending more time on my commute than with my kids each workday. I felt professional guilt for not being "present" for all hours in the office and having to race out the door every day to get my kids. It was a constant, debilitating cycle. What I learned, the hard way, was that guilty feelings will come, but you need to find a way to release them. Imagine an alternative perspective you would share with a friend. Do that for yourself. Focus on what you can control, and what you can't, and work on managing your expectations.

Your career will ebb and flow for various reasons. There is still an opportunity to grow professionally as a working parent or caregiver. Where you are now or what you're worried about now may not look or feel the same five years from now. Take the best care of yourself as you work. Your situation isn't permanent, and if there's a performance issue, you will tackle it. Until then, keep maintaining your career commitments, activating your personal care plan, reviewing and acknowledging your progress, adjusting your next steps, and taking each experience one day at a time.

Q&A

Here are some questions I've been asked concerning talking to your manager about your caregiving situation or parenting needs.

When should I share that I'm having a baby?

Sadly, there isn't a perfect time to share your good news, and that can be agonizing. Some women choose to share in their first trimester, some wait until later; that choice is yours to make. It's a highly personal decision that can also be affected by how your pregnancy is progressing.

In the interim, take time to research and understand your rights for unpaid or paid leave. These vary based on the size and location of your employer and their own policies. Review your employee handbook closely for guidance.

Out of respect to your working relationship, your manager should be the first person to know at your company. If possible, schedule a time to meet. Tell your manager in a face-to-face conversation instead of in e-mail if you can. Don't feel you should have all the details worked out ahead of your first conversation. The two of you can meet again later to discuss next steps.

When the time comes, don't be afraid to ask if you need pregnancy-related work accommodations. It can be intimidating to know how to approach it, but don't be afraid to share the news, or feel apologetic. I'd like you to be confident. This is great news! Any concerns you have about bias or perceptions are completely out of your control, so channel your energy into positive places.

When should I tell my manager about my caregiving responsibilities?

It's always best to let your manager know what's happening if there's a change in circumstances that have the potential to have an impact on your work. If you can, have a conversation in person and follow their cues with regards to how you can problem-solve together.

Almost everyone, at some point in their career, will face a caregiving situation. While it can feel terrifying, as it's personal to you, this is a universal occurrence that no employer is immune to. Remember, your manager may be able to suggest employer resources you were unaware of. There may be workplace benefits that can help you, such as paid or unpaid family leave, paid sick days, flexible workdays, and remote work opportunities. As hard as it seems, telling your manager is the best way to start to navigate next steps.

How much leave should I take if I'm having a baby?

The first thing to do is understand your options and evaluate vacation time available. At the time of writing here in the United States, if you and your employer meet certain requirements, you are guaranteed 12 weeks unpaid leave under the Family and Medical Leave Act. In addition, some states have their own distinct parental leave laws, so you should familiarize yourself on your rights based on your circumstances and location.

Your options for paid or unpaid leave will depend on where you live and the policies of your employer. Some companies have their own parental leave policies, in addition to short-term disability policies. If you have questions about your options, you should talk to an HR professional to make sure you understand everything. Then, consider when you want to return to work, the options you have available, and determine your leave based on those parameters. Remember, there may be options to adjust your plan if needed in the future.

PART III
PIVOT

CHAPTER
7

How to Pull Off
a Career Change

If you could do any job at all, what would it be?

If your answer is, "Octavia, I'm already doing it," that makes me so happy. That's awesome. As a reward, you get to skip this chapter.

For many of us, there comes a moment where we feel like we've hit a wall. And then another. And then one more. Feeling like you're trapped in the wrong career isn't much fun. I've been there. I coach individuals who are trying to break into something new, as well as people who've pivoted more than once. Careers can be a bit quirky, but it can be tough if you feel like yours is completely offbeat.

Are you ready for a reset? According to a study by the job site Indeed, the major factors that drive employees to hit the eject button and change careers are pay, happiness, growth, and professional development.[1] These factors echo what I hear from professionals during my coaching sessions. Feeling unfulfilled, underutilized, and underpaid are the most common forces that result in the decision to make a seismic shift. In addition, the study found that workers spent 11 months on average considering whether to make the leap.[2]

At the start of our career, we usually choose something based on a set of assumptions. Then, when we've picked our path, society tends to put people in boxes. I dislike putting people in boxes because people are full of surprises. Many folks are usually waiting for the right moment to bust out of their box and do something totally unexpected. Luckily, boxes can be recycled. So whatever label you've had based on your line of work can easily be adjusted.

My career history includes delivering newspapers, caring for kids at a day camp, working in retail as a sales associate, directing public relations campaigns, and sitting on the board of a nonprofit organization. Each one of my work experiments and experiences helps me make better career decisions. The variety of my experiments also underscores that I can learn new things. The job titles I've held don't even begin to describe what I learned on the job. I no longer deliver newspapers, and I can't remember how to use a cash register anymore. But what I absorbed remains with me.

Delivering newspapers taught me about time management and efficiency. I learned, often the hard way, about the importance of early rising. If I didn't get up on time and fold the stack of papers I'd received overnight for delivery, I couldn't complete my paper round before I had to get ready for school. That experience is something I leaned on, often without realizing, in every job that followed. To this day, I hold myself accountable to always being prepared and on time for meetings.

During college when I worked as a retail sales associate, I learned about profit and loss for the first time. Our team was guided on how much revenue our store had generated the day before, and the figure we needed to hit that day. I learned how to engage customers and close sales. I still put those skills into practice today as I grow my coaching business.

Your accomplishments and experiences, even in a role or career you are moving on from, can help you as you continue to grow.

Sadly, career choices don't come with a guidebook. We learn from trying things out and making mistakes. It can be hard to pinpoint one thing. You just don't know until you try something, and you may always wonder what an alternate profession might have felt like.

The best-selling novel *The Midnight Library* by Matt Haig is centered on a woman named Nora who bitterly regrets her perceived lack of ambition. Unexpectedly, Nora is offered the opportunity to experience what her life would have been like if she'd pursued contrasting career choices. As it turned out, Nora was brilliant at lots of different things. In the various versions of her life, Nora was a rock musician, a retired Olympic swimmer, a professor, a vineyard owner, an author, and an animal rescuer. Nora's experiences reminded me that we hold so much potential within us, but the only person who can determine what matters is you.

So how do you pull off a career pivot?

Changing direction to try something new can be exciting but terrifying at the same time.

Sometimes a job is a means to an end. It can be a stepping-stone. Or it might be something you've always dreamed of doing. Your jobs can vary greatly and what your work represents can vary at different points in your life too.

However, your career is something you choose to pursue and invest in. The best part is you get to decide. You may be looking to make a shift. You may be looking to make a seismic change.

To pull off a career change, there are four things you need:

- Creative thinking
- Confidence
- Connections
- Commitment

Flexing these four principles will power your momentum to push through and embark on a new career journey. Here's how to do it, starting with using creativity to bust out of the box you're in.

Creative Thinking

When you're a kid, from time to time adults will ask, "What do you want to be when you grow up?" You probably had an answer, or several, to that question. But as a kid, do you know what the working world requires? Not a chance. Do you understand anything about how to find a job? Unlikely. Do you know about the breadth of opportunities that lie ahead of you? Probably not. You may have ideas about what you want to be, based on stuff you like, something you've heard, read, or seen. That's because there's no way to make an informed decision on something we haven't experienced.

The same applies when we become adults. You may know exactly what you want to do, or you may be unsure about what career path to choose. In both cases, we make considerations based on what we know and what we're drawn to, to try things out and see how it works.

Even when you know the career you want to try next, there can still be uncertainty. And that uncertainty can feel destabilizing.

Whatever resources you use to help figure things out, I want to make sure you hold space for your responses to these questions:

1. **What would you love to try?**
2. **What do you want to stop doing?**
3. **What are your must-haves?**

Getting real about what you want, and why you work, is paramount. In chapter 1, Know Your Worth, I shared how to compile your career values and create goals that align with your purpose and principles. When you're preparing for a professional pivot, be clear on what matters most to you by using your responses to the Career Values exercise. Get clear on what you want to change by understanding what isn't working for you and why.

Chapter 1 also shares how to create a career road map. These tools will help you determine your next steps to navigate a career change. Writing down what you want to pursue or explore is an exciting and important milestone. Identifying the initial next steps you need to take sets your intentions for how to move forward. This road map will be the foundation for the adventure you're about to embark on.

When you're trying something new, find ways to keep brainstorming and keep creating ideas as your curiosity grows. Stay in that curious space.

Filter Your Ideas

How do you know what's a great idea and what's not? Is the idea realistic? Is it enough? Can I pull it off? Will I earn enough? These are all valid questions, and they can be tough to answer. To evaluate your ideas, you'll need to consider what matters, what's driving you, and what you want and need.

Wants and needs overlap, but they are not the same thing. Financial planners often ask individuals to prioritize spending based on wants and needs. Sometimes a similar approach can be helpful when it comes to considering career options. So how do you distinguish between a want and a need?

In this context, I define a need as a high-priority necessity that lays the foundation for the career values that matter to you most. I define a want as something you'd love to have or experience in your career.

Review the list of ideas you currently have. Which ideas align with what you *need*? Which ideas align with what you *want*?

For example, the amount you earn is a common primary need. Money matters; it's fundamental for sheer survival. If you don't have a financial safety net to insulate you as you leap into uncertainty, or if you're in a lower salary bracket, it's vital to create a plan based on your needs. When that's the case, knowing the minimum level of compensation you need to hit is essential. What else is on your needs list? Write everything down.

Then, consider the icing on the cake—your wants—because how you earn your money matters too. What are the factors that would make you super excited about a new opportunity? You get to decide what's essential and where you can be flexible.

Let's aim to get both the money you need and the work you want. Being excited by both is infectious.

Aligning What You Have and What You Need

When you've explored what you'd like to pursue, it's time to align what you have, in terms of your skills, and what you need, in terms of resources.

If you like making lists, do that. When I'm trying to piece things together, my go-to are mind maps. I love them because they allow me to visually organize my brain dump of ideas and thoughts.

I'd like you to create a list or a mind map for each of the following questions. You don't need to follow the order. Just start with the first one you're drawn to.

Create a header for your list or draw a circle in the middle of a piece of paper. Write down one of the questions and start throwing down ideas:

- What transferable skills do I have?
- Who do I know that can help me?
- What resources could I explore?
- What groups could I be a part of?
- What will I need to learn?
- Who do I need introductions to?
- What's missing and how could I fix it?

Creative Planning

Aligning what you have and what you need will cement opportunities to pursue in your career road map. This is your career change plan. When it comes to embarking on a career change, your road map becomes even more important because you'll be building out ideas, methods, and approaches you may not have experienced before. In essence, it will require you to be more creative.

What does "be more creative" mean? Well, depending on the career path you're embarking on and how much of a pivot it is, it means thinking differently as you figure out options. This often involves looking at the landscape ahead from multiple angles, drawing on more resources, and asking deeper questions about how you could get to your destination.

For example, if you were to ask me, "Hey Octavia, I trained as an accountant, but I really want to make music videos. What should my next steps be?" I'd ask you some exploratory questions so we could bounce ideas around:

- Do you want to transition gradually, or is this a hard stop?
- Do you need training or further education before you can begin your new career?
- Can you test it out? Could the new profession be a project, volunteer work, or a side hustle at first?
- Is there a way to sidestep into doing more of what you are interested in where you work now?
- Can you do it simultaneously with what you do now?
- What could a next step be?
- What are some of the bigger milestones you anticipate you need to reach?
- What are some of the ways you could build a bridge to where you want to be?

You can use these questions as a basis for your deeper thinking, but you should also add more questions to the mix. Your responses will help determine avenues you can research further or start to pursue. The next step is to ask yourself, "What are three things I could try to move this forward?"

As you create your career road map, picture yourself as an explorer who may discover a new avenue, may meander a bit, or must track back after reaching a dead end. That's okay; there isn't one set path, and the more you try, the further you'll go.

If you need to build experience in your chosen field to demonstrate your worth to a future employer, get creative when it comes to assessing your options. Depending on your needs, they could include:

- Pursuing a degree, either full- or part-time
- Taking a course

- Volunteer work
- Finding a part-time role
- Freelancing
- Applying for internship or returnship programs
- Shadowing someone in the role

By the end of the career road map process, you'll have the start of a plan that can continue to grow.

But what do you do if the ideas you have on paper feel like they belong to an alternate universe? How do you turn hopes, dreams, and ideas into reality?

It's time to assess your confidence.

Ana's Story

"For me, the hardest part was figuring out what to do next. I didn't trust my judgment after crashing and burning in the career I'd chosen. I was underperforming because I hated everything about it. My previous job had been more of the same, and I didn't feel like I had any real achievements to boast about.

"Trying to decide what to do next from a position of weakness was so hard. Plus, I couldn't afford not to work. After what felt like months of misery, I had a frank conversation over drinks with a close friend. She basically told me I could keep doing what I was doing, or I could do something about it. She was right.

"That night I made a list of the kind of work that used to excite me. I hadn't tried those things, but I realized it was something to start with. I picked three options and decided to devote time to learning as much as possible about each one. Every Sunday, I spent time researching companies, looking for job descriptions, making a list of the skills needed, and pulling apart my résumé. I didn't plan to start applying for roles, but one night I saw a job posting that caught my eye. The fact I was drawn to it confirmed

I was moving in the right direction. In that moment I knew I was ready to commit to something new. Just that feeling alone gave me a boost and I felt excited for the first time in forever."

Confidence

Confidence can be such a peculiar thing. When we have it, we are usually blissfully unaware. And I don't mean that we become arrogant—simply that we don't usually think about it at all.

Think about how you operate when you know exactly what you're doing. We don't consider ourselves confident; we just do it. For example, if you learned how to ride a bike, you can usually hop on without really thinking. You just ride. If you're still learning how to ride a bike, however, you'll be wobbling all over the place and beating yourself up for not knowing how to do it yet.

Confidence usually becomes a problem when we feel that our abilities, qualities, judgment, or level of experience are lacking. When you haven't done something before, it feels like starting over, and that can make you feel vulnerable, even when the excitement is there.

So when it comes to our careers, it's not surprising that our confidence can take a ton of hits. Careers can feel competitive, and that's when you already know what you're doing. If you feel like you're starting over, there's a lot of stake. Professionally, financially, and emotionally. It's quite a cocktail.

But here's the thing: to make a career leap, you need to

1. Make the decision;
2. Act on the decision; and
3. Find an employer who believes in you.

And yes, depending on where you are in the process—the start, the middle, or searching for your next employer—this might seem like a monumental leap. But that won't happen unless you do whatever it takes to ramp up your self-confidence. An employer will believe in you if you believe in yourself.

Create a Scary List

When in doubt, look back at what you've handled in the past. Creating a Scary List involves thinking back to times when you've done something frightening or intimidating that you'd never done before. It doesn't necessarily have to be work related; I just want you to list all the things you've done that were super challenging.

Creating a Scary List will remind you of times when you stepped out of your comfort zone and emerged on the other side. Chart what you did and reflect on the steps you took to do it.

- What got in the way?
- How did I figure it out?
- How did it feel when I completed it?

There may be several moments where you will feel that your career change is out of reach. If you feel like that, reflecting on the times when you've done big, bold things in the past will give you a subliminal boost when you might need it most.

Talk Positively About Your New Career

When you've made the decision to pursue something new, the time will come to start telling friends, family, professional connections, and prospective employers. This might not feel easy at first, but the more you do it, the easier it will become. Plus, hearing yourself say the words out loud, and often, reinforces them.

When it's time to start sharing your new career plan, you should practice how to articulate it with confidence. Each conversation will be a little bit different, based on the audience. But I encourage you to be consistent, and of course, when it comes to talking to professional connections and prospective employers, you want to make sure your pitch is authentic, but polished.

I recommend giving some context to explain—in a positive way—why you're making a change. You can highlight relevant skills, experience, and attributes as you explain it.

So instead of saying:

> *"I spent years studying to be a dentist, I hated every second, so I decided to quit and pursue graphic design instead."*

Try this:

> *"I started my career as dentist, and in addition to the technical skills I acquired, my communication skills were a huge asset. I've always been passionate about design, so I started pursuing projects to build my port-folio. I'm excited to use my design skills, coupled with my client service skills, in my next role."*

Steer clear of negativity and focus on what makes you a compelling candidate. Your personal motivators for why you're quitting your old career, such as being unfulfilled or unpaid, won't motivate a potential employer to hire you. However, people will pick up on enthusiasm. It's also your responsibility to connect the dots from your old profession to your new one, with solid examples of skills and experience that are unique to you.

People may be curious or dismissive of your aspirations. Don't let that throw you off. Instead, be ready for the follow-up question. People will want to dig a little deeper, and you're likely to hear something along these lines:

Wow, this is a huge step, why do you want to make such a big change?

Be ready to explain your "why" with conviction. Don't diminish your career journey up to this point. Be proud of all of it. Emphasize enthusiastically how your past experiences and skills will continue to help you succeed.

It's likely that not everyone will understand your decision and that's okay. Focus on connecting with advocates and people with objective perspectives, versus outright naysayers. There will be lots of opinions. Your opinion is the most important of all.

Gravitate toward people who give you room to grow. Get advice from people in your chosen field, but bear in mind that hearing how one person achieved something doesn't mean you have to follow the same path. Even if you tried, you can't replicate someone else's career as it has been shaped by so many factors.

Be Prepared for Lows and Fear of Letting Go

There will be moments where you may feel like you're taking a step backward. You might regret not making the change sooner, or you may start to wonder if it will take you forever to build up gradually to what you want. You may also be wondering what to do with your previous career. Yes, you know you need to leverage the best bits in job interviews, but what do you do with the knowledge you have, the people you met, and all the things you did along the way?

Transitions aren't neat, and all the feelings you will move through are valid. Ultimately you decide your end goals, and even if the goals shift, you'll keep moving forward. A big part of moving forward, regardless of your career choices, is letting go of something. Sometimes, to help my coaching clients process their thoughts around this, I equate a big career change to looking for a new home. Sometimes the move is forced by circumstances, sometimes it's something you've wanted. Finding a new home isn't always straightforward. You may have a wish list, but not everything ticks every box. When you find a place you love, you keep your fingers crossed hoping you'll get it. Sometimes you will, sometimes you won't. When you do make the move, there's upheaval. Often you must figure out what to take and what to leave behind. When you're in the new space, it takes a little while for it to feel like home. Changing careers, especially when it's a big shift, can take a while to execute and more time to adjust to.

When it comes to saying good-bye to your old career, you'll gradually let it go and the best parts will stay with you. The experiences and achievements remain even if you're no longer doing the work daily. And remember, what you did before propelled you to what you choose to do next.

Giving yourself time to navigate your transition is important, and support can often come from unexpected places. Therefore, I want to make sure you don't underestimate the value of connections.

Connections

Often, a coaching client will confess that they hate networking. It feels forced. Making small talk sucks. Bothering people feels awkward. Keeping in touch is tricky. It all feels a bit fake and transactional.

I get it, and while I'm a huge advocate of networking, I know that trying to make professional connections can sometimes feel a bit weird. But the good news is there are lots of ways to connect with others to help with your career change without feeling conflicted about it.

If you're unsure about how to engage with more connections, I'd like you to consider what your needs are, right now. This will help you determine where to focus and prevent you from feeling overwhelmed.

Here are some questions to assess where you are and clarify the best approach:

1. What's my immediate goal when it comes to making connections?
2. How would I describe myself and what I'm doing right now in one to two sentences?
3. Who am I looking to engage with?
4. Where am I visible?
5. What's worked well for me in the past when it comes to meeting and connecting with people?
6. Who do I think is great at putting themselves out there? What can I learn from how they do that?
7. Where do I need to be seen?
8. What's the first thing I could try to connect with more people?
9. What are two other things I could try to make new connections?
10. What's one thing I could do to stay in contact with important connections?

Networking isn't just about working the room at an event or asking your former boss to meet you for a coffee. Even if a connection is fleeting, it can be valuable. A piece of advice you hear on a podcast can be just as useful as if you hear it directly in a one-to-one conversation. A question asked during a workshop can resonate even if you weren't the one to make the ask. A chance conversation with a friend could open an introduction to someone you knew nothing about previously.

If you don't have a mentor, is there a prominent person in the career you're targeting that you admire? If so, follow their work and learn and absorb from a distance. Do they write articles? If so, set up alerts and read their work. Are they active on social media? If so, follow them. Have they written a book? If so, read it. You get the idea.

There are lots of ways to forge connections to inspire you on your new path. Here are some approaches you can try.

Start Career-Focused Conversations

There are two questions I'd love you to answer:

1. Whom do you know who made a major career change?
2. Whom do you know who works in the profession you're exploring?

Make a list for each, and then start to reach out to each person on it. If you're not sure how to make the ask, you could say something like, "I admire how you've pursued your career. If you have time, I'd love to learn more about how you started doing _____."

Don't try to figure out all the steps alone. Talk to as many different people as possible, as conversations will spark ideas. Don't expect that everyone you ask can help with your individual goals, but you might hear something that ignites an idea—and ideas alone are worth their weight in gold.

Conversations may result in introductions, recommendations, referrals, a new mentor, or even informational interviews. You never know where a conversation can take you. Don't bombard people, though. Be selective and thoughtful with your asks.

Build New Networks

If you don't know many people who work in the profession you want to move into, it's time to start building new networks. This takes time, and you can't create this overnight, but it's an investment worth making.

As a first step, you can often find mid- to senior-level professionals who are active on LinkedIn, and it's easy to follow them and observe what they share. You don't have to send a LinkedIn invite to follow their updates. You can also follow recruiters or human resources executives who work in the sectors you're targeting. These groups are usually incredibly active on LinkedIn, as it's such a key talent-acquisition platform, so taking the same approach could uncover useful insights and opportunities.

Ask people you know if they know people who work in the fields you want to explore further. If they do, ask for introductions. It's often not the people you know, but who they know, that can be incredibly helpful. I understand networking doesn't come naturally to everyone. Especially if you feel like you're trying to do something you haven't achieved yet. But as you are building toward something new, that's when talking to others matters most.

Follow the Crowd

Where possible, attend as many events, workshops, and panels related to your new career path as you can, and join relevant groups or networks. These can range from social media groups to professional associations.

Following the crowd allows you to observe and learn from what others share. These types of connections, even if they're not one-on-one conversations, can still be incredibly valuable. They may also help expand your awareness of industry trends or help you frame a question to ask during a job interview. The possibilities are endless.

Christine's Story ━━━━━━━━━━

"The hardest part was telling my family I didn't want to be a paralegal anymore. They were horrified. Their disappointment made me wonder, for the thousandth time, if I was crazy to consider leaving my career behind. They were so focused on what I was leaving behind, they couldn't see how excited I was about the new opportunities I was exploring.

"I'd decided I wanted to use my corporate background with helping nonprofit organizations find grants and funding. Making the transition required a significant pay cut, and that took me some time to research and for me to get comfortable with. I would need to drastically change my lifestyle if I wanted to make it work. On top of that, the friends I confided in warned me that it might be hard to get a job at another law firm if I changed my mind.

"Despite the salary difference and the concerns of people around me, I was quietly confident. I was convinced, because I worked at a big law firm, it would be easy to find a new role. But I was wrong! My job search was so frustrating—each time I found a great role it seemed to go nowhere. It seemed a lot of nonprofits wanted to hire fundraisers who had already worked in that space. Very few people seemed to want to take a chance on interviewing me. But I was determined. It took dozens and dozens of failed applications before I finally got an offer."

Commitment ━━━━━━━━━━

So commitment is the secret sauce that underpins pretty much everything. If you're trying to pull off a career change, you need to be all in. That means being persistent, but also patient. Proactive, but strategic. Authentic, but intentional.

Most of all, I want you to be ambitious. Mentally prepare for the fact you may not always be a match for a role description. That's okay. Don't be afraid to apply for things. What's the worst that can happen?

That sounds a bit exhausting, right? There is a lot to consider and that's before you've polished the tools you'll be using. After you've reviewed this chapter, I encourage you to flip ahead to chapter 9, where you'll find the Dream Bigger Career Toolkit. It's designed to help you create a strong résumé and cover letter to support your career change job search. You will also find pointers to help you prepare for interviews.

Keep Checking Your Road Map

Unfortunately, there isn't a mathematical equation that will predict how long it will take to pivot into a new role. That said, you may have a time line of your own that's paramount.

In addition to reviewing the next steps on your road map, it's important to calculate the investment needed to pursue your career change. This may be the number of hours a week you can devote to further education, or the budget you've assigned to test it out. Whatever you've earmarked, it's important to keep checking and refining as needed. That way you'll know if your actions are moving in the right direction by meeting your needs, or if you need to refocus.

Hold Yourself Accountable

This part can be hard, but a big part of it is deciding "What will I commit to?" Whether that's this week, this month, or this year. I'm a big fan of celebrating mini milestones along the way. There will be so much of your career change that goes unseen by anyone else; people usually only pay attention when you do the big visible thing—land a new job. But getting to that point takes work. People see the before and the after and don't really witness up close the messy middle. All your work, at each step, should be recognized. The person to give that recognition is you.

When I'm embarking on something with lots of steps or stages, one thing I do is plan a set of mini treats. Funnily enough, the reward part is easy to skip over! I often don't feel like I deserve it, but I make myself pause and indulge in the treat I'd preplanned. It's a reminder that I'm building and each step matters.

Dealing with Rejection

When you start applying for jobs, you may find there's a whole lot of silence or you may start to receive rejections. This feels crushing; there's no way to sugarcoat that, but push through it. Take a breath and pull out your career road map. Update some new next steps. Keep talking to and learning from connections as you navigate the job search process.

Don't let a recruiter throw you off if you don't get a response, or if your job application isn't successful. Recruiters are not looking at roles in the same way you are. Recruiters are often looking for the lowest level of risk. You are ready to take the biggest risk and do whatever it takes to push your career forward.

For employers, finding the right fit is more than finding the candidate who has the perfect résumé. Remember, employers hire people to solve problems, and problem solving isn't industry specific.

Create Proof Points

If you get called to interview, this demonstrates on paper you have what it takes to do the role. Congratulations! However, in preparation for interview opportunities, there's some work I'd like you to do.

Be proud of what you've done so far in your career. Keep a list of your accomplishments, skills, and experience and be ready to expand on the proof points in your résumé. In addition, think of other proof points to show your commitment to your new career. These are things you can keep working on throughout your job search process. They could be something you show, such as a portfolio or work you've completed, a testimonial, or a certificate for an accreditation. Or it could be something you share, such as a brief takeaway from a workshop you attended.

Career transitions can take time to complete. As you continue to work through your career road map of next steps, I'd like you to commit to asking yourself these questions on a regular basis:

- Who needs to know what I'm working toward?
- Who needs to know what I'm capable of?
- How can I share that?

If you believe you can do this, your enthusiasm and persistence will be infectious. Be authentic. Take your time and find what feels right for you. Transitions can take years, and it's not a race to the finish. Embrace the fact that every step you take will move you closer to where you want to be.

Remember, lots of things are scary. Staying in a career that's wrong for you is an even bigger risk, because you're putting a ceiling on your potential. Executing a career pivot shows you're not afraid of change. It proves your adaptable, proactive, and multitalented. And those are a set of impressive attributes to have.

Q&A

Here are some questions I've been asked about how to pull off a career change.

How do I know for sure that I'm in the wrong job versus the wrong career?

If something feels wrong, I encourage you to go back to the Career Values exercise in chapter 1 and assess how your current role stacks up against your primary career needs.

It's also important to consider the moment of time you're in. Did your team recently go through organizational changes? How is your company's financial performance? Has your scope of work changed? Identify other factors that might be contributing to how you're feeling right now.

When you've identified the source of the bad feelings, you'll be able to more accurately determine whether it's something specific to your job, or something related to your career. Do your best to be as objective as possible. Also make a list of times when things felt great at work and do the same assessment against your Career Values to determine what made those moments so special, and identify where and how to replicate them.

I've lost interest in my career, but I feel stuck because I've invested so much time already. What should I do?

Careers shift all the time but deciding to make a change is a big deal. It can be scary because the stakes are high. Shifting from what you know to unknown or uncertain territory isn't easy. If you're feeling down about choosing the wrong career, try not to "shoulda, woulda, coulda" the choices that got you to this point. Instead, flip your mindset to embrace what you've uncovered so far, and to prepare yourself mentally to explore something that meets all your needs.

Trying out a career, whether you ended up liking it or not, is a valuable life experience. You only discover what you want to do if you try something out. Outgrowing an experience is more than okay. Your worth is not your tenure in a field you don't want to be in. Hold on to the fact you're a multifaceted, multiskilled individual who could do a lot of awesome things.

Do I need to go back to an entry-level role to start over?

Not necessarily, but this depends on what you're looking to pivot into, and what the requirements are to get started in that role. That said, I always advise trying to identify opportunities to sidestep into your new career.

Talk to friends and connections you trust to brainstorm possible ways you could bridge to where you want to be. Is there an option to take a role within your current company that's more closely aligned with your new career goals? Could you take on a side hustle or other projects to add experience to your résumé before making a leap? Could you transition within your industry sector, so you can bring knowledge you already have to your career path?

As you consider all options and talk to people who work in your chosen career, you'll have a more solid foundation to start considering next steps to explore.

CHAPTER

8

Be Pivotal by Paying It Forward

Paying it forward matters. Sometimes the smallest interaction can pave the way for a career-changing opportunity. At numerous points over the past two decades, thanks to other people's actions and support, I have been recommended for roles, invited to speak at events, and nominated for awards. One of the most powerful tools we can wield is the ability to help others advance. I know from my own experience that the actions of others have opened doors and accelerated my opportunities.

We all know the value of networking when it comes to building your career. However, for minority women, there comes a point where we may feel like we've hit a ceiling. Having friends at work is great and having a manager you work well with is wonderful, but having someone who will champion your work is in an entirely different league. If you don't have an advocate in your corner yet, guess what? You can be a supporter of others by paying it forward. Building a career is hard. I will never forget, and will be forever thankful to, the people who have given me invaluable support.

Often, the individuals who have boosted us during our professional pursuits remain in the background. Their actions often take place behind closed doors and may not be known by many. That's why I love the "Personal Board of Directors" section in the *Wall Street Journal* so much. I have the *Journal* delivered to my house every day, and this section is my favorite to read. It features interviews with business leaders, who in turn highlight the individuals they go to for advice. Each person shares how their mentors and advocates have shaped their perspectives and helped them to succeed at work.

In one interview, Payal Kadakia, the executive chairman and cofounder of ClassPass, discussed how she turns to Anjula Acharia, a serial entrepreneur, tech investor, venture capitalist, and a dance teacher, for advice. Payal recounted how she had just quit a role at Warner Music and had been confused about what to do next. At their first meeting, Anjula asked her: "If you're not willing to bet on yourself, why would anyone else?" That question proved to be a turning point. Her mentor's encouragement was pivotal in helping Payal rally the courage to pursue a new venture.[1]

Another "Personal Board of Directors" interview featured Dr. Erika James, dean of the Wharton School at the University of Pennsylvania, and the first woman and person of color to hold that post in Wharton's 140-year history. Erika shared her speed dial support list, which includes Simmons University President Dr. Lynn Wooten. The two women met when Erika began graduate school, and she describes Lynn as someone who has supported her throughout her career. "She and I are on the phone, and I'm not exaggerating, every day," Erika explained. "We've been able to really support each other for our entire professional journey."[2]

I love the *Wall Street Journal*'s series because it shines a spotlight on what we usually don't see. It demonstrates how a successful career is built on drive, focus, and acumen, coupled with pivotal relationships, valuable support, and moments of inspiration.

This chapter shows how you can be the kind of woman who thrives by amplifying the abilities and accomplishments of others. To get things started, I will share three pay it forward principles. They are approaches you can use to be pivotal to another person's career as you continue to build and grow yours:

1. Do Good Things
2. Use Your Voice
3. Ignite Growth

1. Do Good Things

There are career-enhancing roles that exist outside your day job. If you haven't considering this before, think about options that might be in your immediate orbit. For example, does your company have employee resource groups? Are you a member of a professional association? Is there a nonprofit you've donated to on a regular basis? Is there a cause or organization you're passionate about? If so, it's likely there could be groups, committees, or boards with opportunities for you to get involved in.

Stepping into a leadership role within a group or committee or on a board is a great way to pay it forward. It can also be a career catalyst, as some of the possible benefits include:

■ Using your professional expertise and skills at a senior level to help an organization or company move forward.

- Supporting causes or initiatives that resonate with you.
- Forging new relationships through networking and connections.
- Gaining visibility.
- Enhancing project management and financial management skills.
- Deepening your knowledge of business operations.
- Acquiring broader skills that expand your areas of expertise.
- Contributing to the culture of a company.
- Boosting your résumé.
- Providing peer-to-peer support to others.
- Making a difference and being of service.

Remember, you don't have to say yes to every opportunity to participate in a committee or employee resource group. You don't have to say yes to a request to join a board. It may be a volunteer position, but that doesn't mean you should underestimate the remit and requirements. If it's a paid position, you should still consider the remit and the requirements. Consider whether the opportunity is right for you and your goals by asking yourself the following questions:

What do you want to accomplish on a personal level?

What would you want to accomplish as part of the responsibilities associated with the opportunity?

What attracts you to the opportunity?

What makes you nervous about the opportunity?

How does the opportunity support your career goals?

What are the requirements and duration of the commitment?

If an opportunity isn't right for you, think of someone it could be perfect for. Mellody Hobson, co-CEO and president of

Ariel Investments, shared a fantastic example of recommending someone else for a leadership role. Mellody is a force. She started at Ariel Investments as a summer intern and rose up the ranks to become co-CEO. In addition to leading America's first Black-owned mutual fund, Mellody's résumé includes board roles at Starbucks, JPMorgan Chase, the Rockefeller Foundation, and DreamWorks Animation.

During an interview with James Manyika, cochair and director of the McKinsey Global Institute, Mellody recounted a call she received from Wynton Marsalis. The acclaimed trumpeter, composer, and artistic director of Jazz at Lincoln Center had reached out to ask Mellody to join the board. Her response was: "I cannot do that but I'm going to give you a crazy idea. Take my 28-year-old chief of staff . . . she can handle it. She will be a giant breath of fresh air for you."[3]

The time will come when you're invited to do something good, but it's not the right fit for you. When that happens, recommend someone else. What happens after your suggestion isn't up to you, but it might be a win-win. The worst that can happen is you enhance the visibility of another individual who deserves recognition.

Sharing someone else's accomplishments can also be pivotal. It's great to acknowledge an achievement by congratulating the individual in the moment. Sharing their accomplishments with others is a powerful way to make someone feel seen. That might be sharing kudos in a team meeting. It might be a congratulatory post on your social media. If someone in your network does something amazing, tell other people about it. If someone on your team does something amazing, tell your bosses about it. Whatever channel you choose, when you see great work, recognize it. It will make someone's day and reinforce their attributes to others.

Recommending the work of others is valuable. This might take the form of offering to provide a reference to someone you respect.

Or it might be as simple as writing a LinkedIn recommendation for someone you've worked closely with. Recommendations often happen when the person is unaware of it. However they manifest, recommendations are one of my favorite ways to pay it forward. It's a great way of shining a spotlight on someone else. It's also so easy to do. If someone has impressed you, if they have skills you admire, tell someone else about their work.

One of the influential recommendations someone can make is choosing to nominate another person for an award. The first two awards I received during my career were because I was nominated by someone else. The first award recognition gave me the confidence to continue to pursue the work that I do now. The second award resulted in a long-haul flight and a trip to Buckingham Palace to receive it. In both instances, someone decided to invest in me by nominating me for recognition I would never have considered remotely possible.

The culmination of both experiences resulted in my pay it forward habit: nominating women for recognition. Now, I fully acknowledge that winning awards is subjective. Nominating someone doesn't necessarily mean they will be recognized. After all, there are so many people who deserve applause and a trophy but may not receive it. But demonstrating that you are able and willing to shine a spotlight on someone else matters, regardless of the outcome.

2. Use Your Voice

Have you been in a meeting recently where one person, or small cohort, dominated the conversation and everyone else was pretty much silent? I know, that happens a lot. If you're leading a meeting, make space for broader participation and perspectives. Bring in quieter voices. Ask other people for their opinions, ideas, or suggestions. Use open-ended questions. Give other people your full attention when they are speaking. These are just a few ways you can involve others by using your voice to help others use their voice too.

Another way to use your voice is to invite others to events that could support their professional development. If you're attending an event or a conference, think of other women in your network who may be interested and share it with them. Even if you're not attending, if you see something great, think of someone who might appreciate the tip. People may choose to attend something, or they may choose not to attend. That's ultimately up to them, but knowledge is valuable. Sharing knowledge is one of the simplest ways to pay it forward.

Talking to other women about career goals can create space for an empowering conversation. When was the last time you were asked about your career goals? Or when was the last time you talked to someone else about what they want to pursue? If there are women in your circle who are starting or building their careers, find opportunities to ask them about what they're building toward. Many years ago, I asked a friend about her goals while we were hanging out, and she looked at me in shock. She told me "no one had ever asked her that before." Don't assume people have the space to share what they're building toward. Also, if you're starting a conversation, be ready to be asked about your perspective. You may decide to talk about something you're working toward now, or something you've pursued in the past, and how you navigated that process.

Do you know how much your peers are earning? One of the most important conversations underrepresented women need to have can feel like taboo. And when that taboo is broken, it can make people feel awkward. Janet Mock, the television producer of the FX drama *Pose*, made headlines when she used the podium at the TV show's season premiere to detail her salary and publicly question why she wasn't making more.[4]

I'm all about talking money, even though it's a tricky subject to navigate. Learning from each other about salary figures, bonuses, stock options, and every kind of compensation option propels us all forward. We won't know what we don't know. Talking matters. How can you know if you're making less than you should when you don't know what other people earn?

But I get it. You may not be comfortable sharing your paycheck with anyone who asks. I completely understand that, and there are ways to talk money without sharing every detail. It's empowering for someone more junior than you to hear your perspectives on salary ranges. Even sharing how you have handled compensation conversations is helpful, even if you don't reveal exact numbers. Helping someone gather knowledge and insights will help them consider how to negotiate when the opportunity arises.

PayScale, a compensation data and software company, found that having an advocate at work can make an impact on your pay. In a 2019 salary survey, only 55 percent of Black and Hispanic women reported having a sponsor at work. PayScale's data identified Hispanic and Black women have the most to gain from sponsorship. Hispanic women with a sponsor earn 6.1 percent more than Hispanic women without one. Black women with a sponsor earn 5.1 percent more than Black women without one.[5]

Many of us have not had someone truly advocate for us at work. When you have the opportunity, be that person for someone else.

3. Ignite Growth

One of the things I appreciate the most about my mentor are the suggestions and ideas I never would have thought of. Every conversation opens my mind to new possibilities. You can do the same for someone else. Being a sounding board for ideas can ignite so much. It's easy to underestimate the impact you will have.

Encouragement goes a long way, especially as big, scary goals can take a long time to accomplish. Supporting someone as they are working toward something that matters is meaningful. Writing a book is a lonely process with plenty of moments for self-doubt and procrastination. As I was working on this manuscript, my mentor would text me from time to time to touch base. Even the briefest interactions gave me a boost. After each check-in, I'd jump into working on, or even just thinking about, a next step that would bring this book into existence. It was motivating to have someone in my corner.

Sharing your mistakes can be as powerful as sharing your accomplishments. We all make mistakes, but they are not always visible to others. Mistakes are priceless because that's how we learn. Sharing what we've learned the hard way can help others who are trying to figure out their next steps. Get comfortable with sharing what has and hasn't worked for you.

Facilitating introductions can make a world of difference to a person's career. A thoughtful introduction could lead to a new project, a new mentor, or even a new career opportunity. That doesn't mean you necessarily have to make every single introduction that is asked of you. If a request puts you in an awkward position, you can and should politely decline. This can be hard because we often want to help others. A connection should ideally be advantageous to both parties and be something that cements your existing relationships. You don't want to burn bridges with a constant stream of requests to someone who doesn't really want them. Even if you're happy to make an introduction, it's smart to check that both sides are okay with it before you do it.

Whenever someone approaches me with, "Hey, I know you know so-and-so. Can you connect us?" I consider how well I know each person as a first step. Then, if it feels right and I know each person well enough to consider it, I always check with the other person first. Try to avoid making assumptions. I always recommend reaching out to ask if that's something they're comfortable with and provide as much context as possible.

I've had embarrassing experiences where I made an introduction and then the person didn't follow through. I learned from those experiences to only make introductions when I know and respect the individual making the ask and our relationship is strong enough for me to trust they will follow through and be professional. If you're thoughtful and intentional about introductions, this may mean there are times you say no, and that's totally fine. Trust your instincts. When you're thoughtful and intentional about connecting people for mutual benefit, it can be a game changer.

In chapter 4 we discussed the importance of mentors and advocates if you're positioning yourself for a promotion. Now's the time to consider how to fill that role for someone else. Doing so reinforces your attributes as a leader, even if you may feel you're still growing and learning, and reinforces your commitment to the advancement of others.

So what's the difference between a mentor and an advocate? In essence, a mentor is reactive; they share their experiences and answer your questions. An advocate is proactive; they make things happen for you using their influence to create new opportunities for you.

A mentor might discuss their career journey and suggest strategies for your professional development. An advocate would help set up a meeting that could get you your next role. A mentor might explain how they secured a promotion. An advocate will recommend you to senior leaders for a promotion. A mentor will tell you what they did, or what you could do. An advocate will act on your behalf and use their influence to help you advance.

The next generation of women following in our path will need support. Become a mentor. Advocate for someone else. Be the person you would have benefited from knowing at the start of your career.

The roles of mentor and advocate can overlap. You may be supporting someone who works at your company, or someone outside your organization. You may even be reverse mentoring someone more senior than you are. This is when a junior professional mentors a senior professional to exchange knowledge, perspectives, and skills. There are no hard-and-fast rules. You can maximize your impact in whichever role you choose.

- Ask questions.
- Avoid making assumptions.
- Be honest.
- Provide constructive feedback.
- Be an active listener.
- Provide a safe space for difficult conversations.
- Maintain confidentiality.
- Be ready to embrace new perspectives.
- Don't be attached to always being right.
- Be accountable.
- Be proactive.
- Be invested.

It's not possible to do it all, and you may not be able to help everyone who approaches you, but even small actions to pay it forward can be truly pivotal. Use your experience to answer questions. Use your network to help open doors. Use your perspective to help raise the bar higher. Listen, support, develop, promote, nurture, recommend, encourage, amplify. Let's propel others forward as we continue to grow in our careers.

Q&A

Here are some questions I've been asked about paying it forward.

What if I don't feel experienced enough to be a mentor?

You can be a mentor at any stage of your career. There will always be someone who can learn from your experiences of building your career so far. Don't be afraid to share what you know with others. Don't be afraid to share your mistakes.

Think about when you were at school. How much you would have benefited if you had been able to talk to your future self. You can pay it forward as an alumna by going back to your school or college and sharing your career journey so far.

Being a good mentor involves being a good listener. You don't need to have the perfect career to be a good mentor. Remember that someone else's journey may not be the same as yours, but they will still benefit from having you as a sounding board. You can use your position as a mentor to ask thoughtful questions to help your mentee gain perspective on what they can do next.

Reflect on the women who inspire you. Do they know how you feel? Unless you've told them so, it's likely they do not. Remember, it's more than likely you are a role model to others, and you may not even realize it.

It feels weird to talk publicly about my achievements. How do I get past that?

Outside of job interviews or performance reviews, there often aren't many opportunities where we get the chance to share what we've accomplished. As a result, it's not uncommon for it to feel weird to talk publicly about your career highlights. But don't let that throw you off. If you have the opportunity, whether it's on a speaking engagement or a media interview, share your achievements with confidence. Even if you have to fake the confidence part.

Your accomplishments are facts, not embellishments. You're not showing off, you're not bragging—you're sharing your skills and expertise. Remember, your achievements may help others set new goals as well as learn from your experience. Using your voice is one of the most powerful ways to pay it forward.

Someone asked me for a testimonial, but I don't know what to write. What should I do?

In essence, a testimonial is a personal recommendation of someone's abilities, skills, and character. If you're comfortable and happy to provide a testimonial, but you're not sure what to share, you can always ask the person requesting the recommendation to share a draft with you for you to review. That way you can see exactly what they were looking for and edit it along the lines of what you're comfortable with.

Remember, less is often more. A testimonial doesn't necessarily have to be long for it to be valuable. One to three sentences will work just fine. In essence, a testimonial explains the work someone has done for you and what made it exceptional. Briefly explain the context of your working relationship, what the person delivered, and what makes them stand out.

Networking feels so transactional and fake. How can I feel more comfortable doing it?

I understand, and you're not alone in feeling that way. A lot of people feel uncomfortable networking, but keep in mind that it's essentially just getting to know more people.

At best, networking is a two-way process where you can help others, gain valuable insights, connect with inspiring people, and identify opportunities along the way. Building a network is important for your career, but it's equally important to maintain your network in a way that's authentic to you. There isn't a perfect formula for this, and it's not something that you can do overnight.

Find what feels right for you. Always be considerate of other people's time. You can't help everyone, and not everyone in your network may be able to help you right now, but you're making an investment in your future. Growing relationships takes time. Cultivating a circle of close contacts that you respect is worth substantially more than accumulating scores of social media followers you may barely know.

Don't overlook the people you already know, and make the time to reconnect. Keeping in touch makes a difference— this can vary from reaching out every so often, to checking in on how they are, to arranging a time to meet for coffee. When it comes to relationships and connections, quality is always better than quantity. Set an intention of networking actions you will take, rather than focusing on the outcome. We can't control the outcome of our actions, but we can control what we do.

9

Dream Bigger Career Toolkit

U se the worksheets, checklists, and resources in this chapter to tackle the obstacles that stand between you and your next career milestone.

In this chapter, you will find the following:

My Career Values Worksheet

Career Road Map Worksheet

Job Search Worksheet

Cover Letter Checklist

Résumé Revisions Checklist

Over 300 Action Verbs to Leverage on Your Résumé

Interview Preparation Checklist

My Career Growth Plan Worksheet

My Career Commitments Worksheet

Recommended Resources

My Career Values

Your career values are your guiding light, in good times and tough times. The following 15 questions provide a space for you to cement your career values.

1. What matters the most to me personally when it comes to my career?

2. What's on my must-have list when it comes to the work I do next?

3. What makes me feel excited and inspired about my work?

4. What motivates me to do my best work?

5. What am I naturally good at?

Figure 9.1a

My Career Values

What would I love to do more of at work?

What energizes and excites me?

What type of environments do I want to work in?

What's my preferred work schedule?

Is there anything that's nonnegotiable for me at work?

Figure 9.1b

My Career Values

What are the greatest accomplishments of my career so far?

What is it about these accomplishments that make them special to me?

What do I want my career to feel like?

What do I want to be known for?

How do I measure success?

Figure 9.1c

Career Road Map

Use your career values and goals to create your own road map.

_____

MY CAREER VALUES

_____

MILESTONE MOMENTS

_____

SHORT-TERM GOALS

_____

LONGER-TERM GOALS

_____

HOW TO PROGRESS

_____

HOW TO CELEBRATE

_____

Figure 9.2

Job Search Worksheet

Gather ideas, actions, connections, and resources to power your job search.

RÉSUMÉ REVIEWERS

LINKEDIN PROFILE REVIEWERS

REFERENCE TARGETS

INFORMATIONAL INTERVIEW TARGETS

Figure 9.3a

Job Search Worksheet

Gather ideas, actions, connections, and resources to power your job search.

NETWORKING TARGETS

INTERVIEW PREP HELPERS

SALARY NEGOTIATION HELPERS

IDEAS TO EXPLORE FURTHER

Figure 9.3b

Cover Letter Checklist

☐ Use a confident, positive, and professional tone.

☐ Create a concise, impactful introduction, referencing the position you are applying for.

☐ Emphasize why you are interested in the role.

☐ Detail your most relevant skills using the keywords from the job application.

☐ Highlight a key accomplishment, using action verbs, to demonstrate your alignment with the role.

☐ Thank the employer for their consideration.

☐ Include your contact information.

☐ Ask someone to proofread your final draft.

Figure 9.4

Résumé Revisions Checklist

☐ Keep it clear, concise, and easy to read.

☐ Align skills and achievements with the job description.

☐ Make sure the professional experience summaries are relevant for the role.

☐ Use the keywords referenced in the job description.

☐ Quantify your achievements.

☐ Amplify your achievements with action verbs.

☐ Print out and proofread multiple times, with multiple people.

Figure 9.5

Here's a list of over 300 action verbs you can leverage for your resume.

Accelerated	Assessed	Classified	Converted
Accomplished	Assigned	Coached	Conveyed
Achieved	Attained	Coded	Convinced
Acquired	Audited	Collaborated	Coordinated
Acted	Authored	Collected	Corrected
Adapted	Authorized	Combined	Corresponded
Addressed	Awarded	Communicated	Counseled
Adjusted	Balanced	Compared	Created
Administered	Began	Compiled	Critiqued
Advanced	Blocked	Completed	Cultivated
Advertised	Boosted	Composed	Curated
Advised	Briefed	Computed	Customized
Advocated	Built	Conceptualized	Debated
Aligned	Calculated	Condensed	Debugged
Allocated	Campaigned	Conducted	Decided
Amplified	Capitalized	Conferred	Defined
Analyzed	Captured	Conserved	Delegated
Appointed	Cataloged	Considered	Delivered
Appraised	Categorized	Consolidated	Demonstrated
Approved	Centralized	Constructed	Described
Arbitrated	Chaired	Consulted	Designed
Arranged	Championed	Contacted	Detected
Articulated	Charted	Contracted	Determined
Assembled	Clarified	Controlled	Developed

Figure 9.6

Devised	Established	Fostered	Integrated
Diagnosed	Estimated	Founded	Interacted
Directed	Evaluated	Furnished	Interpreted
Discovered	Examined	Furthered	Interviewed
Discussed	Exceeded	Gained	Introduced
Dispatched	Executed	Gathered	Invented
Displayed	Expanded	Generated	Investigated
Distributed	Expedited	Guided	Involved
Documented	Experimented	Handled	Itemized
Drafted	Explained	Headed	Joined
Drew	Explored	Hired	Judged
Drove	Expressed	Hosted	Launched
Earned	Extracted	Identified	Lectured
Edited	Fabricated	Illustrated	Leveraged
Educated	Facilitated	Implemented	Lifted
Elicited	Fashioned	Improved	Listened
Eliminated	Fielded	Incorporated	Lobbied
Emphasized	Filed	Increased	Located
Enabled	Finalized	Influenced	Logged
Enforced	Forecasted	Informed	Maintained
Engineered	Forged	Initiated	Managed
Enhanced	Formalized	Inspected	Mapped
Enlisted	Formed	Inspired	Marketed
Ensured	Formulated	Installed	Maximized
Entertained	Fortified	Instituted	Measured

Figure 9.6 (*Continued*)

Mediated	Performed	Recommended	Restructured
Mentored	Persuaded	Reconciled	Retrieved
Merged	Photographed	Recorded	Revamped
Mobilized	Pioneered	Recruited	Reviewed
Modeled	Planned	Rectified	Revised
Moderated	Predicted	Redesigned	Revitalized
Modified	Prepared	Reduced	Saved
Monitored	Presented	Referred	Scheduled
Motivated	Presided	Refined	Screened
Navigated	Printed	Refocused	Scrutinized
Negotiated	Prioritized	Registered	Searched
Observed	Processed	Regulated	Secured
Obtained	Produced	Rehabilitated	Shaped
Operated	Programmed	Reinforced	Showcased
Orchestrated	Projected	Remodeled	Simplified
Ordered	Promoted	Renovated	Solicited
Organized	Proposed	Reorganized	Solved
Originated	Provided	Repaired	Sparked
Outlined	Publicized	Replaced	Spearheaded
Outpaced	Published	Reported	Specialized
Outperformed	Purchased	Researched	Specified
Overhauled	Qualified	Reserved	Standardized
Oversaw	Quantified	Resolved	Steered
Participated	Raised	Responded	Stimulated
Partnered	Reached	Restored	Streamlined

Figure 9.6 (*Continued*)

Strengthened	Sustained	Trained	Verified
Studied	Systematized	Transformed	Volunteered
Succeeded	Targeted	Unified	Won
Summarized	Taught	United	Wove
Supervised	Terminated	Updated	
Surpassed	Tested	Upgraded	
Surveyed	Tracked	Utilized	

Figure 9.6 (*Continued*)

Interview Preparation Checklist

☐ Research the company, the role, and the people you will be meeting with.

☐ Prepare and practice your "tell me about you" elevator pitch.

☐ Prepare and practice responses to common and difficult interview questions.

☐ Prepare a list of thoughtful end-of-interview questions about the role or the company.

☐ Review your list of achievements and most relevant skills.

☐ Ask a friend to conduct a practice interview.

☐ Plan and prep your interview outfit.

☐ Pick the best environment for a phone or video interview.

Figure 9.7

My Career Growth Plan

In the first column, pick an area or skill you want to develop to advance your career.

Consider the obstacles that stand in the way of this, and jot those down in the second column.

Finally, use the third column to brainstorm ways to move past the obstacles.

Skills I want to develop	Obstacles	Solutions

Figure 9.8

My Career Commitments

Your career commitments are your personal pledges. You will create them based on your unique needs, and use them to anchor how you move forward.

I'm doing this work because . . .

To do my best work and feel like I'm thriving, I need to . . .

Figure 9.9a

My Career Commitments

When I hit an obstacle, I will remember . . .

_____

The work I'm doing is laying the foundation for me to . . .

_____

Figure 9.9b

Recommended Resources

American Association of University Women (AAUW)

Founded in 1881, AAUW is a nonpartisan, nonprofit organization committed to advancing gender equity for women and girls through research, education, and advocacy.

aauw.org

Catalyst

Founded in 1962, Catalyst is a global nonprofit that works with companies around the world to accelerate women into leadership.

catalyst.org

Center for American Progress

The Center for American Progress is an independent nonpartisan policy institute that is dedicated to improving the lives of all Americans.

americanprogress.org

Glassdoor

Glassdoor combines the latest jobs with millions of company ratings and reviews, CEO approval ratings, salary reports, interview reviews, and benefits reviews.

glassdoor.com

Harvard Business Review

Through its flagship magazine, books, and digital content, *Harvard Business Review* aims to provide professionals around the world with rigorous leadership insights and best practices.

hbr.org

Indeed

Get an estimated calculation of how much you should be earning and insight into your career options with Indeed's salary calculator.

indeed.com

Institute for Women's Policy Research (IWPR)

IWPR is a nonpartisan, nonprofit organization that engages in research and dissemination to shape public policy and improve the lives and opportunities of women from diverse backgrounds.

iwpr.org

Ladies Get Paid

Ladies Get Paid provides tools, resources, events, and community to help women negotiate for equal pay and power in the workplace.

ladiesgetpaid.com

Management Leadership for Tomorrow (MLT)

MLT is a national nonprofit that is committed to transforming the leadership pipelines of leading organization, enabling talented underrepresented minorities to get on, and stay on, the path to senior leadership.

mlt.org

National Partnership for Women & Families

The national, nonprofit, nonpartisan organization is committed to changing policy and culture. The National Partnership for Women & Families focuses on issues that increase equity, health, and economic justice and how they affect women's ability to thrive and fully participate in our society.

nationalpartnership.org

National Committee on Pay Equity

Founded in 1979, the National Committee on Pay Equity is a coalition of women's and civil rights organizations, associations, coalitions, and individuals working to achieve pay equity.

pay-equity.org

PayScale

PayScale, a compensation data, services, and software company, provides data that allows employees to research their worth in the job market.

payscale.com

Salary.com

The compensation market data, software, and analytics company helps individuals understand their worth and plan their next career move.

salary.com

Step Up

Step Up propels girls living or going to school in underresourced communities to fulfill their potential by empowering them to become confident, college-bound, career-focused, and ready to join the next generation of professional women.

suwn.org

References

Chapter 1

1. "Women of Color in the United States: Quick Take," Catalyst, March 19, 2020, https://www.catalyst.org/research/women-of-color-in-the-united-states/.
2. "U.S. Senator Kamala Harris Speaks at Spelman," Sisters Chapel, Spelman College, October 26, 2018, https://www.spelman.edu/about-us/news-and-events/kamala-harris/page-4.
3. Sheila Brassel, Joy Ohm and Dnika J. Travis, "Allyship and Curiosity Drive Inclusion for People of Color at Work" (Catalyst, 2021), https://www.catalyst.org/reports/allyship-curiosity-employees-of-color/.
4. Amber Burton, "Women of Color: Invisible, Excluded and Constantly 'On Guard,'" *Wall Street Journal*, October 15, 2019, https://www.wsj.com/articles/women-of-color-invisible-excluded-and-constantly-on-guard-11571112060.
5. Nicole Chavez and Faith Karimi, "California Becomes the First State to Ban Discrimination Based on Natural Hairstyles," CNN, July 3, 2019, https://www.cnn.com/2019/07/03/us/california-hair-discrimination-trnd/index.html.
6. Hahna Yoon, "How to Respond to Microaggressions," *New York Times*, March 3, 2020, https://www.nytimes.com/2020/03/03/smarter-living/how-to-respond-to-microaggressions.html.
7. Yoon, "How to Respond to Microaggressions."
8. Pauline Rose Clance and Suzanne Imes, "The Imposter Phenomenon in High Achieving Women: Dynamics and Therapeutic Intervention," *Psychotherapy: Theory, Research & Practice*, 1978.

Chapter 2

1. "At-Will Employment—Overview," National Conference of State Legislatures, April 15, 2008, https://www.ncsl.org/research/labor-and-employment/at-will-employment-overview.aspx.
2. "Labor Laws and Issues," United States Government, access date February 27, 2020, https://www.usa.gov/labor-laws#item-35277.
3. "What Is the Difference Between a Furlough, a Layoff and a Reduction in Force?," Society for Human Resource Management, access date February 26, 2020, https://www.shrm.org/resourcesandtools/tools-and-samples/hr-qa/pages/furloughlayoffreductioninforce.aspx
4. "What Is the Difference Between a Furlough, a Layoff and a Reduction in Force?"
5. "What Is the Difference Between a Furlough, a Layoff and a Reduction in Force?"
6. "Wrongful Termination," FindLaw, access date February 27, 2020, https://employment.findlaw.com/losing-a-job/wrongful-termination.html.
7. "How Do I File for Unemployment Insurance?" US Department of Labor, access date February 26, 2020, https://www.dol.gov/general/topic/unemployment-insurance.
8. Jonathan A. Segal, "Legal Trends: Severance Strategies," Society for Human Resource Management, July 1, 2008, https://www.shrm.org/hr-today/news/hr-magazine/pages/0708legaltrends.aspx.

Chapter 3

1. Kate Erbland, "Octavia Spencer Says LeBron James Helped Her Negotiate Appropriate Pay on Netflix Series—Sundance," *IndieWire*, January 26, 2019, https://www.indiewire.com/2019/01/octavia-spencer-lebron-james-pay-netflix-1202038554/.
2. "Salary and Compensation Statistics on the Impact of COVID-19," Randstad, access date December 29, 2020, https://rlc.randstadusa

.com/for-business/learning-center/future-workplace-trends/randstad-2020-compensation-insights.

3. Anthony P. Carnevale, Nicole Smith, and Artem Gulish, "Women Can't Win: Despite Making Educational Gains and Pursuing High-Wage Majors, Women Still Earn Less Than Men," Georgetown University Center on Education and the Workforce, 2018, https://cew.georgetown.edu/cew-reports/genderwagegap/#resources.

4. Carnevale, Smith, and Gulish.

5. "Despite Increased Labor Force Participation Among Women, Gender Wage Gap Persists, Even in the Occupations They Dominate," The Institute for Women's Policy Research, March 24, 2020, https://iwpr.org/media/press-releases/despite-increased-labor-force-participation-gender-wage-gap-persists/.

6. Robin Bleiweis, "Quick Facts About the Gender Wage Gap," Center for American Progress, March 24, 2020, https://www.americanprogress.org/issues/women/reports/2020/03/24/482141/quick-facts-gender-wage-gap/.

7. "Survey: 55 Percent of Workers Negotiated Pay with Last Job Offer," Robert Half, February 13, 2019, https://www.prnewswire.com/news-releases/survey-55-percent-of-workers-negotiated-pay-with-last-job-offer-300792725.html.

8. "Average Cost-per-Hire for Companies Is $4,129, SHRM Survey Finds," Society for Human Resource Management, August 3, 2016, https://www.shrm.org/about-shrm/press-room/press-releases/pages/human-capital-benchmarking-report.aspx.

9. "Average Cost-per-Hire for Companies Is $4,129, SHRM Survey Finds."

10. "The Next Evolution of Transparent Salaries: Our New Remote-First Formula and Updated Salary Calculator," Buffer, December 6, 2017, https://buffer.com/resources/salary-formula/.

11. "AAUW Worksmart Online Workbook," American Association of University Women, Inc., 2018, https://www.aauw.org/resources/programs/salary/.

Chapter 4 ▨▨▨▨▨▨▨▨▨▨▨▨▨▨▨▨▨▨▨▨▨

1. Working Mother Research Institute, "On the Verge: How to Stop the Tidal Wave of Multicultural Women Fleeing Corporate America," July 22, 2020, https://www.workingmother.com/multicultural-women-gender-gap-report.

Chapter 5 ▨▨▨▨▨▨▨▨▨▨▨▨▨▨▨▨▨▨▨▨▨

1. Rachel Thomas, Marianne Cooper, Gina Cardazone, Kate Urban, Ali Bohrer, Madison Long, Lareina Yee, Alexis Krivkovich, Jess Huang, Sara Prince, Ankur Kumar, and Sarah Koury, "Women in the Workplace: 2020," McKinsey & Company and LeanIn.org, 2020, https://wiw-report.s3.amazonaws.com/Women_in_the_Workplace_2020.pdf.
2. Michael Madowitz, "Calculating the Hidden Cost of Interrupting a Career for Child Care," Center for American Progress, June 21, 2016, https://www.americanprogress.org/issues/early-childhood/reports/2016/06/21/139731/calculating-the-hidden-cost-of-interrupting-a-career-for-child-care/.
3. "The Hidden Cost of a Failing Child Care System," Center for American Progress, access date December 30, 2020, http://interactives.americanprogress.org/childcarecosts/.
4. "Paid COVID-19 Leave Extended on a voluntary Basis Through March 31," *The National Law Review*, December 28, 2020, https://www.natlawreview.com/article/paid-covid-19-leave-extended-voluntary-basis-through-march-31.
5. Megan Leonhardt, "3 Tips to Help You Get Through Losing Your Job, from Someone Who Was Laid Off During the Recession," CNBC, April 15, 2020, https://www.cnbc.com/2020/04/15/3-lessons-tiffany-aliche-learned-that-helped-after-losing-her-job.html.
6. Figures calculated using "The Hidden Cost of a Failing Child Care System," Center for American Progress, access date December 30, 2020, http://interactives.americanprogress.org/childcarecosts/.

7. "Chapter 5: Balancing Work and Family," Pew Research Center, December 11, 2013, https://www.pewsocialtrends.org/2013/12/11/chapter-5-balancing-work-and-family/.
8. "Policy Brief: The Impact of COVID-19 on Women," United Nations, April 9, 2020, https://www.unwomen.org/-/media/head-quarters/attachments/sections/library/publications/2020/policy-brief-the-impact-of-covid-19-on-women-en.pdf.

Chapter 6

1. "Paid Family and Medical Leave: A Racial Justice Issue—and Opportunity," National Partnership for Women and Families, August 2018 https://www.nationalpartnership.org/our-work/resources/economic-justice/paid-leave/paid-family-and-medical-leave-racial-justice-issue-and-opportunity.pdf.
2. "Caregiving in the United States 2020," AARP and National Alliance for Caregiving, May 2020. https://www.aarp.org/content/dam/aarp/ppi/2020/05/executive-summary-caregiving-in-the-united-states.doi.10.26419-2Fppi.00103.003.pdf.

Chapter 7

1. "Career Change Report: An Inside Look at Why Workers Shift Gears," Indeed, October 30, 2019, https://www.indeed.com/lead/career-change
2. "Career Change Report: An Inside Look at Why Workers Shift Gears."

Chapter 8

1. Joann S. Lublin, "The Mentors Helping ClassPass Founder Payal Kadakia Find the Right Steps," *Wall Street Journal*, October 31, 2020, https://www.wsj.com/articles/the-mentors-helping-classpass-founder-payal-kadakia-find-the-right-steps-11604116805.

2. Francesca Fontana, "Who Taught Wharton's Business School Dean Some Important Life Lessons," *Wall Street Journal*, January 16, 2021, https://www.wsj.com/articles/who-taught-whartons-business-school-dean-some-important-life-lessons-11610773250.

3. "A Happy Warrior: Mellody Hobson on Mentorship, Diversity, and Feedback," McKinsey Global Institute, June 18, 2020, https://www.mckinsey.com/featured-insights/diversity-and-inclusion/a-happy-warrior-mellody-hobson-on-mentorship-diversity-and-feedback.

4. Alyssa Morin, "*Pose* Star Janet Mock Gives Impassioned Speech About Salary, Infidelity and More," E! Online, May 1, 2021, https://www.eonline.com/news/1264926/pose-star-janet-mock-gives-impassioned-speech-about-salary-infidelity-and-more.

5. "Sponsors: Valuable Allies Not Everyone Has," PayScale, July 31, 2019, https://www.payscale.com/data/mentorship-sponsorship-benefits.

Acknowledgments

This book would not exist without the support of so many pivotal people to whom I'm forever grateful.

Thank you Jeanenne Ray, Chloé Miller-Bess, Sally Baker, Dawn Kilgore, Purvi Patel, Allegra Green, Paul McCarthy, and the wonderful Wiley team for bringing this book to life.

Leigh Eisenman, my brilliant literary agent at Wolf Literary Services. Thank you for your commitment to this book during the craziest of times and for all the guidance along the way. Gillian MacKenzie, thank you so much for the introduction to Leigh and for championing *Prep, Push, Pivot*.

Adaobi Obi Tulton, my developmental editor at Serendipity23 Editorial Services, working with you has been the standout highlight of my pandemic year. Thank you so much.

Thank you, Donna J. Weinson, my copyeditor, for working your magic on my manuscript.

Heidy Vaquerano, my entertainment attorney at Fox Rothschild, thank you for being such an incredible advocate.

Chenille Sharpe, you make impossible things happen. I don't know how, but you do, and I'm so thankful to have you on the Twenty Ten Agency team.

Laura Rodriguez, thank you for teaching me so much and for continually pushing me out of my comfort zone. I'm so fortunate to have your guidance.

Natalie Mulford, thank you for sharing your expertise, connections, and support for this book.

Henry Timms, you have championed me at every single step. Thank you for opening so many doors and for making time to answer all of my questions.

Ellen Bailey, you are the epitome of paying it forward. Heartfelt thanks. It's always a joy working with you.

Angela Belassie, Simone Byrne, Stephanie Zhong, Eban Howell, and John Pollono, thank you for your continuous encouragement from the beginning of this adventure.

Emily DaSilva, I don't think you realize just how often the tea saved me! Thank you for your gift.

Michael Bungay Stanier, not only did you write my favorite book (*Do More Great Work*), your invites to Cocktails and Conversations gave me so much solace during our crazy Covid summer. Thank you for all the wonderful advice you shared as I embarked on this journey.

David Burkus, Dolly Chugh, Ellen DaSilva, Genelle Aldred, Matthew Bishop, and Jon Denn, thank you for candidly sharing what it takes to become an author.

A bunch of brilliant minds jumped in to review chapters at various stages. A special shout-out to Natalie Reeves, Sara Campbell, Courtney Seiter, Shoku Amirani, and September Rea. Thank you so much.

Robert Diggs, Emily Chiappinelli, and Alexa Clay at RSA US, many thanks for your continuous support. It means the world to me.

Joe Tang, Ariana Gaitan, and Keith Yang at BizHaus, thank you for the beautiful workspace and for your warmth and kindness. I wrote this book in the Haus! I will never forget that.

To the Twenty Ten Agency community of coaches, clients, and friends, I can't thank you enough. It's so rewarding to spend my days with so many incredible people.

A huge thank you to my family, far and wide, for your love and support. I'm indebted to you all.

And finally, to the trio who are the epicenter of everything. Ivan, Thalia, and Marisa, thank you for giving me the space and time to write this book, thank you for making me laugh, and thank you for being my motivation and inspiration.

About the Author

Octavia Goredema is a career coach and the founder of Twenty Ten Agency. Her mission is to help underrepresented professionals advance their careers. Octavia has coached leaders at renowned companies, including Google, American Airlines, Tinder, General Motors, Nike, and Dow Jones.

An acclaimed career expert, Octavia's insights have been featured in the *Harvard Business Review*, *Black Enterprise*, and *Los Angeles Times*, among others. Octavia was appointed a Member of the Order of the British Empire by the Queen in recognition of her work. She is a Fellow of the Royal Society of Arts, where she leads the Gender Equity network in the United States. Originally from England, Octavia lives in Los Angeles, California.

Index

Page numbers: Figures and Tables given in *italics*.